15-MINUTE
ARABIC
LEARN IN JUST 12 WEEKS

Marion Sarhaan

REVISED EDITION
DK LONDON
Senior Editor Ankita Awasthi Tröger
Senior Art Editor Clare Shedden
Illustrator Dan Crisp
Managing Editor Carine Tracanelli
Managing Art Editor Anna Hall
US Editor Mika Jin
US Executive Editor Lori Hand
Production Editor Robert Dunn
Senior Production Controller Poppy David
Jacket Design Development Manager Sophia MTT
Associate Publishing Director Liz Wheeler
Art Director Karen Self
Publishing Director Jonathan Metcalf

DK DELHI
Project Editor Nandini D Tripathy
Project Art Editor Anukriti Arora
Assistant Art Editor Sulagna Das
Managing Editor Soma B Chowdhury
Senior Managing Art Editor Arunesh Talapatra
Senior Jacket Designer Suhita Dharamjit
Senior Jackets Coordinator Priyanka Sharma Saddi
DTP Designers Rakesh Kumar,
Mrinmoy Mazumdar, Nityanand Kumar
Hi-res Coordinator Neeraj Bhatia
DTP Coordinator Vishal Bhatia
Production Manager Pankaj Sharma
Pre-production Manager Balwant Singh
Senior Picture Researcher Sumedha Chopra
Picture Research Manager Taiyaba Khatoon
Creative Head Malavika Talukder

**Language content for Dorling Kindersley by
g-and-w publishing.
Additional translations for 2024 edition by
Andiamo! Language Services Ltd.**

This American Edition, 2024
First American Edition, 2009
Published in the United States by DK Publishing
1745 Broadway, 20th Floor, New York, NY 10019

Contents

How to use this book

This book teaches the Egyptian spoken dialect of Arabic. Twelve themed chapters are broken down into five daily 15-minute lessons, allowing you to work through four teaching units and one review unit each week. The lessons cover a range of practical themes, including leisure, business, food and drink, and travel. A reference section at the end contains a menu guide, an English-to-Arabic dictionary, and a guide to the Arabic script, grammar, and dialects.

Warm up
Each day starts with a warm up that encourages you to recall vocabulary or phrases you have learned previously.

Instructions
Each exercise is numbered and introduced by instructions that explain what to do. In some cases additional information is given about the language point being covered.

Text styles
Distinctive text styles differentiate Arabic, English, and the pronunciation guide.

Audio
This icon indicates that you should listen to audio recordings in order to do the exercise. See page 7 for details of how to access and use the audio app.

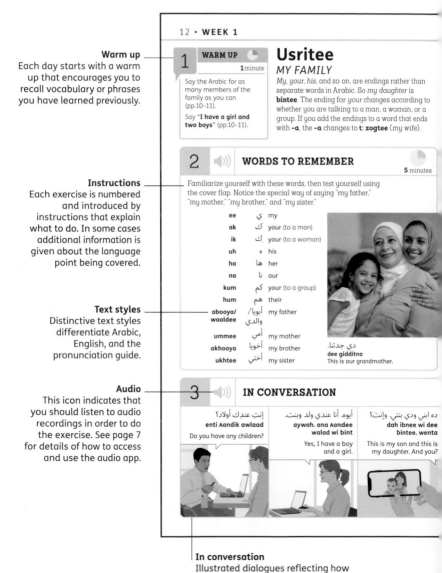

12 · WEEK 1

1 WARM UP
1 minute

Say the Arabic for as many members of the family as you can (pp.10–11).

Say "**I have a girl and two boys**" (pp.10–11).

Usritee
MY FAMILY

My, your, his, and so on, are endings rather than separate words in Arabic. So *my daughter* is **bintee**. The ending for *your* changes according to whether you are talking to a man, a woman, or a group. If you add the endings to a word that ends with **-a**, the **-a** changes to **t: zogtee** (*my wife*).

2 WORDS TO REMEMBER
5 minutes

Familiarize yourself with these words, then test yourself using the cover flap. Notice the special way of saying "my father," "my mother," "my brother," and "my sister."

ee	ي	my
ak	كَ	your (to a man)
ik	كِ	your (to a woman)
uh	ه	his
ha	ها	her
na	نا	our
kum	كم	your (to a group)
hum	هم	their
abooya/ waaldee	أبويا/ والدي	my father
ummee	أمي	my mother
akhooya	أخويا	my brother
ukhtee	أختي	my sister

دي جدتنا.
dee gidditna
This is our grandmother.

3 IN CONVERSATION

إنتِ عندك أولاد؟
enti Aandik awlaad
Do you have any children?

أيوه. أنا عندي ولد وبنت.
aywah. ana Aandee walad wi bint
Yes, I have a boy and a girl.

ده ابني ودي بنتي. وإنتَ؟
dah ibnee wi dee bintee. wenta
This is my son and this is my daughter. And you?

In conversation
Illustrated dialogues reflecting how vocabulary and phrases are used in everyday situations appear throughout the book.

Know your dialect There are more than 20 countries in the Middle East and North Africa (MENA) region, stretching from northwest Africa well into Asia, where Arabic is the official language. The formal language of the media and government across these countries is Modern Standard Arabic (MSA) but informal spoken Arabic varies from region to region. It is spoken Arabic that you will need to use in everyday situations such as shopping and sight-seeing. The Arabic taught in this book is the Egyptian spoken dialect. As Egypt is the region's leading exporter of popular culture in the form of movies, television programs, and songs, the dialect is one of the most widely understood throughout the Arab world. However, since MSA is used in formal written Arabic, the script section at the end of the book is in MSA (p.152).

INTRODUCTIONS · 13

Conversational tip Dah is masculine and can mean *this (is)* or *that (is)*; the feminine equivalent is **dee**. You may also hear these pronounced as **haadah** and **haadee** in other dialects. You can ask a question by simply raising the pitch of your voice at the end of a statement: **dee bintak?** *(is that your daughter?)*; **dah ibnuh?** *(is this his son?)*.

Cultural/Conversational tip
These panels provide additional insights into life in the MENA region and language usage.

4 ◄)) USEFUL PHRASES

3 minutes

Learn these phrases, then test yourself using the cover flap.

Do you have any siblings? (to a man)	إنتَ عندَك اخوات؟ **enta Aandak ikhwaat**
Do you have any siblings? (to a woman)	إنتِ عندِك اخوات؟ **enti Aandik ikhwaat**
This is my husband.	ده زوجي. **dah zoogee**
This is my wife.	دي زوجتي. **dee zogtee**
Is that your sister? (to a man)	دي أختَك؟ **dee ukhtak**
Is that your sister? (to a woman)	دي أختِك؟ **dee ukhtik**

Exercises
Familiarizing you with terms relevant to each topic, these help you build your vocabulary, learn useful phrases, connect words to visuals, and practice what you learn.

4 minutes

أيوه. أنا عندي ولدين.
aywah. ana Aandee waladein
Yes. I have two boys.

5 SAY IT

2 minutes

Do you have any siblings? (to a woman)
Do you have any children? (to a man)
I have two sisters.
This is my father.
Is that your mother? (to a woman)

Time yourself
The icon and text to the right of the heading show you how long you need to spend on each exercise.

Say it
In these exercises you are asked to apply what you have learned using different vocabulary.

»

Review

The cover flaps enable you to review what you learn in each unit by testing yourself as you go. At the end of every week's lessons, a review unit tests what you've learned so far. A recap of selected elements from previous lessons helps to reinforce your knowledge.

Learn
Keep the flaps open while you learn.

Review
Use the flaps to cover the answers when you are ready to test yourself.

Reference

This section appears at the end of the book and brings together all the words and phrases you have learned over the weeks. While the menu guide focuses on food and drink, the dictionary lists Arabic translations of common words and phrases.

Dictionary
Mini-dictionary provides ready reference from English to Arabic for 2,000 words.

Menu guide
Use this guide as a reference for food terminology and popular Arabic dishes.

SPECIAL SOUNDS

Many of the pronunciations in Arabic are similar to English equivalents (pp.152–153), but some require emphatic and guttural sounds which are not found in English:

h/H   Arabic has two **h** sounds: **h** as in *horse*, and a second sound (**H**) from the epiglottis, forcing air out as if breathing on glasses to clean them.

s/S   There are two **s** sounds: a soft **s** as in *silly*, and a hard **S** as in *saw*.

d/D   There are two **d** sounds: **d** as in *ditch*, and **D**, with the tongue touching the palate.

t/T   There are two **t** sounds: a soft **t** as in *twitch*, and a heavy **T**, with the tip of the tongue touching the alveolar ridge, as in *Tokyo*.

z/Z   There are two **z** sounds: **z** as in *zebra*, and **Z**, which is more voiced.

a/A   There are two **a** sounds: **a** like the **u** in *butter*, and **A**, a guttural sound from the back of the throat, pronounced by dropping the **n** in **-ein**.

g/j   Pronounced **g** as in *good* in Egyptian Arabic, but **j** as in *jug* in more formal MSA.

kh   A throaty **h**, with the tongue root touching the palate, as in the Scottish *loch*.

gh   Similar to **kh**, but produced from the back of the throat, like the French **r**.

'   A short pause or glottal stop as when the **tt** in *butter* is dropped.

q   A heavier version of **k** in formal MSA, with the back of the tongue touching the soft palate. This is dropped in Egyptian Arabic, turning **qahwa** (*coffee*) into **ahwa**. In other regions, it is a hard **g**, turning **qahwa** into **gahwa**.

oo   A common vowel sound in Egyptian Arabic, as in *four*.

ei   A common vowel sound in Egyptian Arabic, as in *great*.

HOW TO USE THE AUDIO APP

The free audio app accompanying this book contains audio recordings for all numbered exercises on the teaching pages, except for the Warm Up and Say It exercises (look out for the audio icon). There is no audio for the review pages.

To start using the audio with this book, download the **DK 15 Minute Language Course** app on your tablet or smartphone from the App Store or Google Play and select your book from the list of available titles. Please note that this app is not a stand-alone course, but is designed to be used together with the book to familiarize you with the language and provide examples for you to repeat aloud.

There are two ways in which you can use the audio. The first is to read through the 15-minute lessons using just the book, then go back and work with the audio and the book together. Or you can combine the book and the audio from the start, pausing the app to read the instructions on the page.

You are encouraged to listen to the audio and repeat the words and sentences out loud until you are confident you understand and can pronounce what has been said. Remember that repetition is vital for language learning. The more often you listen to a conversation or repeat an oral exercise, the more the new language will sink in.

SUPPORTING AUDIO
This icon indicates that audio recordings are available for you to listen to.

FREE AUDIO APP

1 WARM UP
1 minute

The Warm Up panel appears at the beginning of each topic. It will remind you of what you have already learned and prepare you for moving ahead with the new subject.

Ahlan
HELLO

Arabs are generally very effusive on meeting. The wide variety of greetings are often accompanied by back-slapping, handshakes, hugging, and kissing. However, it is best to avoid physical contact with the opposite sex on first meeting to avoid causing any unintentional offense.

2 WORDS TO REMEMBER
2 minutes

Familiarize yourself with these words by reading them aloud several times, then test yourself by concealing the Arabic on the left with the cover flap.

صباح الخير **sabaaH il-kheir**	Good morning
صباح النور **sabaaH in-noor**	Good morning (reply)
مساء الخير **masaa il-kheir**	Good afternoon/evening
مساء النور **masaa in-noor**	Good afternoon/evening (reply)
تشرّفنا **tasharrafna**	Pleased to meet you
شكرا (جزيلاً) **shukran (gazeelan)**	Thank you (very much)
مع السلامة. **maA as-salaama**	Goodbye

أهلاً!
ahlan
Hello!

3 IN CONVERSATION: FORMAL
3 minutes

صباح الخير.
أنا اسمي مايك هولند.
sabaaH il-kheir. ana ismee mike holland

Good morning. My name is Mike Holland.

صباح النور.
أنا اسمي أمينة هاشم.
sabaaH in-noor. ana ismee ameena haashim

Good morning. My name is Amina Haashim.

.انفـرّشت
tasharrafna

Pleased to meet you.

4 PUT INTO PRACTICE

3 minutes

Read the Arabic on the left and follow the instructions to complete this dialogue. Then test yourself by concealing the Arabic on the right with the cover flap.

مساء النور.
masaa in-noor

مساء الخير.
masaa il-kheir

Good evening.

Say: Good evening. (reply)

تشرّفنا.
tasharrafna

أنا اسمي أمير زكي.
ana ismee ameer zaki

My name is Amir Zaki.

Say: Pleased to meet you.

Cultural tip

A polite way to address someone is to use **yaa** before their name when speaking to them directly—for example, **marHaba yaa Sami** (*hello Sami*). This is not used when you are talking about someone else, someone who is not present during the conversation, or someone you are not speaking to directly.

5 USEFUL PHRASES

3 minutes

Learn these phrases by reading them aloud several times, then test yourself by concealing the Arabic on the right with the cover flap.

What's your name? (m/f) — ما اسمَك/ اسمِك؟
ma esmak/esmek

My name is... — أنا اسمي...
ana ismee...

See you soon. (m/f) — أشوفَك على خير/ أشوفِك على خير
ashoofak Ala kheir/ ashoofik Ala kheir

---

6 IN CONVERSATION: INFORMAL

3 minutes

سلام يا سامي!
salaam yaa saamee

Bye, Sami!

مع السلامة.
أشوفك بكرة.
maA as-salaama. ashoofik bokra

Goodbye. See you tomorrow.

مع السلامة.
maA as-salaama

Goodbye.

1 WARM UP
1 minute

Say "**hello**" and "**goodbye**" in Arabic (pp.8–9).

Now say "**My name is...**" (pp.8–9).

Say "**Pleased to meet you**" (pp.8–9).

Il-Aela
RELATIVES

In Arabic, relatives are categorized according to whether they are related to the mother (maternal) or the father (paternal). For example, the maternal uncle and aunt are **khaal** and **khaala**; the paternal uncle and aunt are **Aamm** and **Aamma**. Cousins are referred to by the precise relationship: **ibn khaal** (*son of maternal uncle*), and so on.

2 🔊 MATCH AND REPEAT
5 minutes

Look at the people in this scene and match their numbers to the vocabulary list on the left. Then test yourself by concealing the Arabic on the left using the cover flap.

❶ جدة
gidda

❷ جد
gidd

❸ أب
ab

❹ أم
umm

❺ بنت
bint

❻ ابن
ibn

❼ أخ
akh

❽ أخت
ukht

❶ grandmother
grandfather ❷
❸ father
❹ mother
daughter ❺
❻ son
❼ brother
❽ sister

Cultural tip In Arabic, things as well as people are masculine (m) or feminine (f). Words referring to women end mostly, but not always, in **-a**—for example, **gidda** (*grandmother*). Feminine things also often end with **-a**—for example, **kursee** (*chair*) is masculine, while **ahwa** (*coffee*) is feminine; however, **shams** (*sun*), which ends in a consonant, is also feminine.

3 WORDS TO REMEMBER:
RELATIVES
4 minutes

زوجة
zooga
wife

زوج
zoog
husband

أنا متجوز/ة
ana mitgawwiz/-a
I'm married (m/f).

Familiarize yourself with these words, then test yourself using the cover flap.

father-in-law	حمى **Hama**
mother-in-law	حماة **Hamat**
children	أولاد **awlaad**
I have four children.	أنا عندي أربع أولاد. **ana Aandee arbaA awlaad**
I have a boy and three girls.	أنا عندي ولد وثلاث بنات. **ana Aandee walad wi talat banaat**

4 WORDS TO REMEMBER:
NUMBERS
3 minutes

Familiarize yourself with these words, then test yourself using the cover flap.

Arabic plurals need to be learned individually. For example, the plural of **bint** (*girl*) is **banaat**; the plural of **walad** (*boy*) is **awlaad**, also used to mean *children*. When numbers are used with plurals, they lose the final **-a** when put directly in front of another word, as in **talat banaat** (*three girls*).

A feature of Arabic is the "dual" ending. When talking about two of something, you don't usually use the number two, **itnein**. Instead you put **-ein** on the end of the word: **bintein** (*two girls*).

one	واحد **waaHid**
two	اثنين **itnein**
three	ثلاثة **talaata**
four	أربعة **arbaAa**
five	خمسة **khamsa**
six	ستة **sitta**
seven	سبعة **sabAa**
eight	ثمانية **tamanya**
nine	تسعة **tisAa**
ten	عشرة **Aashra**
zero	صفر **Sefr**

5 SAY IT
2 minutes

I have two boys.

I have three children.

I have a brother and two sisters.

Usritee
MY FAMILY

1

WARM UP
1 minute

Say the Arabic for as many members of the family as you can (pp.10–11).

Say "**I have a girl and two boys**" (pp.10–11).

My, your, his, and so on, are endings rather than separate words in Arabic. So *my daughter* is **bintee**. The ending for *your* changes according to whether you are talking to a man, a woman, or a group. If you add the endings to a word that ends with **-a**, the **-a** changes to **t: zogtee** (*my wife*).

---

2 **WORDS TO REMEMBER**

5 minutes

Familiarize yourself with these words, then test yourself using the cover flap. Notice the special way of saying "my father," "my mother," "my brother," and "my sister."

ee	ي	my
ak	كَ	your (to a man)
ik	كِ	your (to a woman)
uh	ه	his
ha	ها	her
na	نا	our
kum	كم	your (to a group)
hum	هم	their
abooya/ waaldee	أبويا / والدي	my father
ummee	أمي	my mother
akhooya	أخويا	my brother
ukhtee	أختي	my sister

دي جدتنا.
dee gidditna
This is our grandmother.

---

3 **IN CONVERSATION**

إنتِ عندِك أولاد؟
enti Aandik awlaad

Do you have any children?

أيوه. أنا عندي ولد وبنت.
aywah. ana Aandee walad wi bint

Yes, I have a boy and a girl.

ده ابني ودي بنتي. وإنتَ؟
dah ibnee wi dee bintee. wenta

This is my son and this is my daughter. And you?

Conversational tip Dah is masculine and can mean *this* (is) or *that* (is); the feminine equivalent is **dee**. You may also hear these pronounced as **haadah** and **haadee** in other dialects. You can ask a question by simply raising the pitch of your voice at the end of a statement: **dee bintak?** (*is that your daughter?*); **dah ibnuh?** (*is this his son?*).

---

4 USEFUL PHRASES

3 minutes

Learn these phrases, then test yourself using the cover flap.

Do you have any siblings? (to a man)	إنتَ عندَك اخوات؟ **enta Aandak ikhwaat**
Do you have any siblings? (to a woman)	إنتِ عندِك اخوات؟ **enti Aandik ikhwaat**

This is my husband.	ده زوجي. **dah zoogee**
This is my wife.	دي زوجتي. **dee zogtee**

Is that your sister? (to a man)	دي أختَك؟ **dee ukhtak**
Is that your sister? (to a woman)	دي أختِك؟ **dee ukhtik**

---

4 minutes

أيوه. أنا عندي ولدين.
aywah. ana Aandee waladein

Yes. I have two boys.

5 SAY IT

2 minutes

Do you have any siblings? (to a woman)

Do you have any children? (to a man)

I have two sisters.

This is my father.

Is that your mother? (to a woman)

Yikoon wi Aand
TO BE AND TO HAVE

<table>
<tr><td>

1 | **WARM UP**
1 minute

Say **"See you tomorrow"** (pp.8–9).

Say **"I'm married"** (pp.10–11), **"I have a brother"**, and **"This is my wife"** (pp.12–13).

</td><td>

In Arabic, the verb **yikoon** means *to be*, but it is usually omitted in the present tense. So, *he is from Egypt* is **howwa min maSr** (literally *he from Egypt*). For *I have*, *he has*, and so on, Arabic uses the word **Aand** (*at*) with one of the possessive endings (p.12), as in **ana Aandee akh** (*I have a brother*).

</td></tr>
</table>

2 🔊 **PRONOUNS**

5 minutes

Practice the Arabic pronouns and the sample sentences, then test yourself using the cover flap.

ana	أنا	I [am] (m/f)
enta	إنتَ	you [are] (m)
enti	إنتِ	you [are] (f)
howwa	هو	he [is]
heyya	هي	she [is]
eHna	إحنا	we [are]
entum	إنتم	you [are] (pl)
humma	همّا	they [are]

أنا بريطانية.
ana briTaaneyya
I'm British.

إنتَ/إنتِ منين؟ **enta/enti minein**	Where are you from? (to a man/woman, informal)

إنتم منين؟ **entum minein**	Where are you from? (to a couple or group, informal)

إحنا من مصر. **eHna min maSr**	We're from Egypt.

3 AAND: TO HAVE

5 minutes

Practice **Aand** (*to have*) and the sample sentences, then test yourself using the cover flap. The pronoun is optional: (**ana**) **Aandee** (*I have*), (**howwa**) **Aanduh** (*he has*), etc.

I have (m/f)	أنا عندي
	ana Aandee
you have (m)	إنتَ عندَك
	enta Aandak
you have (f)	إنتِ عندِك
	enti Aandik
he has	هو عنده
	howwa Aanduh
she has	هي عندها
	heyya Aandaha
we have	إحنا عندنا
	eHna Aandina
you have (pl)	إنتم عندكم
	entum Aandukum
they have	همّا عندهم
	humma Aanduhum

عندكم ورد أحمر؟
Aandukum ward aHmar
Do you have red roses?

He has a meeting.	هو عنده اجتماع.
	howwa Aanduh igtimaaA
Do you have a cell phone? (to a man)	إنتَ عندَك موبايل؟
	enta Aandak mubayil
How many brothers and sisters do you have? (to a woman)	إنتِ عندِك كام أخ وأخت؟
	enti Aandik kaam akh w-ukht

4 NEGATIVES

4 minutes

A simple way to make sentences negative in Arabic is to use the word **mish** (*not*). The negative of (**ana**) **Aandee** is (**ana**) **mAandeesh** (*I don't have*). Read these sentences aloud, then test yourself using the cover flap.

ماعنديش عربية.
mAandeesh Aarabyya
I don't have a car.

I'm not British. (m/f)	أنا مش بريطاني/بريطانية.
	ana mish briTaanee/ briTaaneyya
He's/She's not vegetarian.	هو/هي مش نباتي/نباتية.
	howwa/heyya mish nabaatee/nabaateyya
Are you (pl) not from Egypt?	إنتم مش من مصر؟
	entum mish min maSr
I don't have a sister.	أنا ماعنديش أخت.
	ana mAandeesh ukht
I don't have children.	أنا ماعنديش أولاد.
	ana mAandeesh awlaad

RaagiA wi karrar
REVIEW AND REPEAT

il-agweba *Answers*
(Cover with flap)

How many?

❶ ثلاثة
talaata

❷ تسعة
tisAa

❸ أربعة
arbaAa

❹ اثنين
itnein

❺ ثمانية
tamanya

❻ عشرة
Aashra

❼ خمسة
khamsa

❽ سبعة
sabAa

❾ ستة
sitta

---

1 HOW MANY?

2 minutes

Say these numbers in Arabic, then test yourself using the cover flap.

3 ❶
9 ❷
4 ❸
2 ❹
8 ❺
10 ❻
5
7 ❼
6 ❾
❽

Hello

❶ صباح النور. أنا اسمي...
**sabaaH in-noor.
ana ismee...**

❷ تشرّفنا.
tasharrafna

❸ أنا عندي ولدين. وأنتم؟
**ana Aandee
waladein.
wentum**

❹ مع السلامة.
أشوفك بكرة.
**maAasalaama.
ashoofik bokra**

---

2 HELLO

4 minutes

You are talking to someone you have just met. Join in the conversation, replying in Arabic following the numbered English prompts.

sabaaH il-kheir. ana ismee ameena haashim
❶ Good morning. My name is... [your name].

dah zoogee
❷ Pleased to meet you.

enta Aandak awlaad?
❸ Yes, I have two boys. And you?

Aandina bintein
❹ Goodbye. See you tomorrow.

3 TO HAVE

5 minutes

Fill in the blanks with the correct form of
Aand (*to have*).

❶ ana _____ akh

❷ eHna _____ Aarabyya

❸ enta _____ awlaad?

❹ humma _____ ward
aHmar?

❺ howwa _____ mubayil

❻ heyya _____ waladein

❼ entum _____ ikhwaat?

To have

❶ عندي
Aandee

❷ عندنا
Aandina

❸ عندَك
Aandak

❹ عندهم
Aanduhum

❺ عنده
Aanduh

❻ عندها
Aandaha

❼ عندكم
Aandukum

4 RELATIVES

4 minutes

Name these family members in Arabic.

❶ grandmother   grandfather ❷

❸ father   ❹ mother

❺ daughter   ❻ son

Relatives

❶ جدة
gidda

❷ جد
gidd

❸ أب
ab

❹ أم
umm

❺ بنت
bint

❻ ابن
ibn

Fil-kafiterya
IN THE COFFEE HOUSE

<table><tr><td>

1 **WARM UP**

1 minute

Count to ten (pp.10–11).

Remind yourself how to say "**hello**" and "**goodbye**" (pp.8–9).

Ask "**Do you** (plural) **have any children?**" (pp.14–15).

</td></tr></table>

Traditional Arab cafés (**il-ahwa**), once mainly male-oriented, offer Arabic coffee or black tea, finger foods such as **falaafel** (*deep-fried chickpea balls*) or **fool** (*mashed fava beans*), **shisha** (*hookah or water pipes*), and perhaps a game of backgammon or dominoes. Modern coffee houses cater to all ages and genders. Table service is common, and it is usual to tip the server a percentage of the bill.

2 🔊 WORDS TO REMEMBER

Familiarize yourself with these words, then test yourself using the cover flap.

جُلاش
gollash
baklava

قهوة بدون حليب
ahwa bidoon Haleeb
black coffee

شاي بحليب
shaay bi-Haleeb
tea with milk

شاي مع نعناع
shaay maA naAnaaA
mint tea

ساندوتش
sandawitsh
sandwich

فول وطعمية
fool wetaAmyya
fava beans and falafel

سكّر
sukkar
sugar

قهوة بحليب
ahwa bi-Haleeb
coffee with milk

3 🔊 IN CONVERSATION

آخذ قهوة بحليب من فضلك.
aakhud ahwa bi-Haleeb min faDlak

I'll have a coffee with milk, please.

حاجة ثانية؟
Haaga tanya

Anything else?

عندكم بسبوسة؟
Aandukum basboosa

Do you have basboosa [semolina cake]?

Cultural tip Traditionally, coffee is served in a small cup and is black and very strong. Brewed in a special jug, it comes in three basic styles: **saada** (*without sugar*), **mazboot** (*medium sweet*), and **ziyaada** (*very sweet*).

5 minutes

ملبن
malban
Turkish delight

4 **USEFUL PHRASES** **5** minutes

Learn these phrases, then test yourself using the cover flap.

آخذ شاي بدون حليب.
aakhud shaay bidoon Haleeb

I'll have a black tea.

حاجة ثانية؟
Haaga tanya

Anything else?

عندكم فول؟
Aandukum fool

Do you have fool [mashed fava beans]?

كام الحساب؟
kaam il-Hisaab

How much is the bill?

4 minutes

أيوه، عندنا.
aywah. Aandina
Yes, we do.

شكرا. كام الحساب من فضلك؟
shukran. kaam il-Hisaab min faDlak
Thank you. How much is the bill, please?

متين جنيه، من فضلك.
metein gineih, min faDlak
Two hundred pounds, please.

1 WARM UP
1 minute

Ask **"How much is that?"** (pp.18–19).

Say **"I don't have a brother"** (pp.14–15).

Ask **"Do you have fava beans?"** (pp.18–19).

Fil-maTAam
IN THE RESTAURANT

There are a variety of eating places in the Arab world. Traditional vendors and **Aarabyat Akl** (*food stands*) sell popular street foods like **falaafel**, **hawawshi** (*stuffed pita*), **fool**, grilled **kofta** (*minced meat*), and **shawerma** (*roast meat*). Modern restaurants offer more substantial meals, including vegetarian dishes such as **maHshee** (*stuffed vegetables*), fish, meat, and poultry. Dinner is busier than lunchtime.

2 MATCH AND REPEAT
5 minutes

Match the numbered items to the list, then test yourself using the cover flap.

❶ فنجان
fingaan

❷ كاس
kaas

❸ شوكة
shooka

❹ سكينة
sikkeena

❺ معلقة
maAla'ah

❻ طبق
Taba'

❼ فوطة
foo-Ta

cup ❶   wineglass ❷

❸ fork   ❺ spoon
knife ❹   plate ❻   napkin ❼

3 IN CONVERSATION

اهلا. ترابيزة لأربعة، من فضلك.

ahlan. tarabeeza li-arbaAa min faDlik

Hello. A table for four, please.

عندكم حجز؟

Aandukum Hagz

Do you have a reservation?

أيوه، بإسم مبروك.

aywah. bi-ism mabrook

Yes, in the name of Mabrook.

4 WORDS TO REMEMBER

3 minutes

Familiarize yourself with these words, then test yourself using the cover flap.

menu	المنيو **il-menu**
starters	مقبلات **muqabbelaat**
main course	الطبق الرئيسي **iT-Taba' ir-rayeesee**
dessert	الحلو **il-Helew**
breakfast	الفطار **il-fiTaar**
lunch	الغداء **il-ghada**
dinner	العشاء **il-Asha**

بتغذى مع أسرتي
batghada maAa Usritee
I'm having lunch with my family.

5 USEFUL PHRASES

2 minutes

Learn these phrases, then test yourself using the cover flap.

What desserts do you have?	عندكم إيه حلو؟ **Aandukum eh Helew**
The bill, please.	الحساب من فضلك. **il-Hisaab, min faDlak**

4 minutes

تحب تختار أي ترابيزة؟
teHeb tekhtar ay tarabeeza?
Which table would you like?

جنب لشباك،من فضلك.
ganb ish-shibaak, min faDlik
Near the window, please.

اتفضلوا هنا.
itfaDDaloo hina
This way, please.

1 WARM UP

1 minute

Say "**She's British**" and "**They're from Egypt**" (pp.14–15).

Ask "**Do you have a fork?**" (pp.20–21).

Ask "**Do you have mint tea?**" (pp.18–19).

Il-aᴛbaa'

DISHES

Dishes vary from region to region in the Arabic-speaking world, and while each region has its own specialities, much of the cooking is grilled or stewed. There are still not many restaurants that offer a fully vegetarian or vegan menu, but there are several traditional Arabic dishes that do not contain meat or can be prepared without it. Ask your server for advice.

2 MATCH AND REPEAT

4 minutes

Match the numbered items to the list, then test yourself using the cover flap.

❶ خضار
khuᴅaar

❷ فواكه
fawaakih

❸ جبنة
gibna

❹ مكسرات
mikassaraat

❺ شوربة
shorba

❻ فراخ
firaakh

❼ رُز
ruz

❽ سمك
samak

❾ مأكولات بحرية
ma'koolaat baᴴaryya

❿ لحمة
laᴴma

❶ vegetables
fruit ❷
❸ cheese
nuts ❹
soup ❺
❻ chicken
rice ❼
fish ❽
❾ seafood
meat ❿

Cultural tip In the Middle East you can make a whole meal out of bread (**Aeish**) and starters such as **falaafel** (*deep-fried chickpea balls*), **fool** (*fava beans mashed with oil*), **ᴴummus** (*cooked and blended chickpeas*), and many more.

3 WORDS TO REMEMBER: COOKING METHODS

3 minutes

Familiarize yourself with these words, then test yourself using the cover flap.

	fried	مقلي **ma'lee**
	grilled	مشوي **mashwee**
	roasted	في الفرن **fil-furn**
	boiled	مسلوق **masloo'**
	in tomato sauce	بالصلصة **bis-salsa**

ممكن لحمة مشوية؟
mumkin laHma mashweyya
Can I have grilled meat?

4 WORDS TO REMEMBER: DRINKS

3 minutes

Familiarize yourself with these words, then test yourself using the cover flap.

تمر هندي
tamr hindi
tamarind drink

	(mineral) water	مياه (معدنية) **mayya (maAdaneyya)**
	wine	نبيذ **nibeedh**
	beer	بيرة **beera**
	juice	عصير **Aaseer**

5 USEFUL PHRASES

2 minutes

Learn these phrases, then test yourself using the cover flap.

I'm a vegetarian. (m/f)	أنا نباتي/ نباتية. **ana nabaatee/** **nabaatyya**
I'm allergic to nuts.	عندي حساسية من المكسرات. **Aandee Hasasyya men** **el-mikassaraat**
What is mahshee?	المحشي عبارة عن إيه؟ **elmaHshee Aubara** **Aan eh?**

6 SAY IT

2 minutes

What is "kosharee"?

I'm allergic to seafood.

Can I have juice?

1 WARM UP
1 minute

What are "**breakfast**," "**lunch**," and "**dinner**" in Arabic? (pp.20–21).

Say "**I**," "**you**" (masculine), "**you**" (feminine), "**he**," "**she**," "**we**," "**you**" (plural), "**they**" (pp.14–15).

Aawiz
TO WANT

In this section, you will learn an essential verb—**Aawiz** (*to want*)—as well as a useful polite phrase, **mumkin** (*can I have?*). Remember to use this form when requesting something because **ana Aawiz** (*I want*) may sound too strong. If it is clear who you are referring to, you can drop the pronoun: **Aawiz ahwa?** (*do you want coffee?*). Use **Aawza** for a woman and **Aawzeen** for groups.

2 **AAWIZ**: TO WANT

6 minutes

Practice **Aawiz** (*to want*) and the sample sentences, then test yourself using the cover flap.

أنا عاوز/عاوزة **ana Aawiz/Aawza**	I want (m/f)
إنت عاوزة **enta Aawiz**	you want (m)
إنت عاوزة **enti Aawza**	you want (f)
هو عاوز **howwa Aawiz**	he wants
هي عاوزة **heyya Aawza**	she wants
احنا عاوزين **eHna Aawzeen**	we want
إنتم عاوزين **entum Aawzeen**	you want (pl)
همّا عاوزين **humma Aawzeen**	they want

هو عاوز لبن **howwa Aawiz laban**	He wants milk.
هي مش عاوز قهوة **heyya mish Aawiz ahwa**	She doesn't want coffee.

همّا عاوزين شوكولاتة؟
humma Aawzeen shokolaata
Do they want chocolates?

Conversational tip The Arabic phrase **min faDlak** (*please*) literally means *from your grace*: **min** means *from*, and **faDl** means *grace*. The ending **-ak** means *your* when talking to a man (pp.12–13). When talking to a woman, use the ending **-ik (min faDlik)** and, when talking to a group, use **-ukum (min faDlukum).**

3 POLITE REQUESTS

4 minutes

You can use **mumkin...?** (literally *possible...?*) to mean *can I/we have...?*, adding **min faDlak** (*please*) to make your request sound more polite. Practice the sample sentences, then test yourself using the cover flap.

Can I have a juice, please?
(asking a man)

ممكن عصير، من فضلك؟
mumkin Aaseer, min faDlak

Can I have a table for tonight, please?
(asking a woman)

ممكن ترابيزة الليلة، من فضلك؟
mumkin tarabeeza il-leila, min faDlik

Can we have the menu, please?
(asking a group)

ممكن المنيو، من فضلكم؟
mumkin il-menu, min faDlukum

4 PUT INTO PRACTICE

4 minutes

Complete this dialogue, then test yourself using the cover flap.

مساء الخير. عندك حجز؟
masaa il-kheir. Aandak Hagz

Good evening. Do you have a reservation?

Say: No, but can I have a table for three, please?

لا، بس ممكن ترابيزة لثلاثة، من فضلك؟
laa, bass mumkin tarabeeza li-talaata, min faDlak

حاضر. عاوز أي واحدة؟
HaaDir. Aawiz ayya waaHda

Certainly. Which one do you want?

Say: Near the window, please.

جنب الشباك، من فضلك.
ganb ish-shibaak, min faDlak

RaagiA wi karrar
REVIEW AND REPEAT

At the table

❶ مكسرات
mikassaraat

❷ سكر
sukkar

❸ مأكولات بحرية
ma'koolaat baHaryya

❹ لحمة
laHma

❺ كاس
kaas

This is my…

❶ دي زوجتي.
dee zogtee

❷ ده زوجها؟
dah zogha

❸ دي بنتنا.
dee bintina

❹ ده ابنَك؟
dah ibnak

Can I have…

❶ ممكن قهوة بالحليب؟
mumkin ahwa bi-Haleeb

❷ ممكن جُلاش؟
mumkin gollash

❸ ممكن قهوة بدون حليب؟
mumkin ahwa bidoon Haleeb

❹ ممكن ملبن؟
mumkin malban

---

1   AT THE TABLE

Name these items in Arabic.

❶ nuts

sugar ❷

❸ seafood

meat ❹

wineglass ❺

---

2   THIS IS MY…

4 minutes

Say these sentences in Arabic.

❶ This is my wife.

❷ Is that her husband?

❸ That's our daughter.

❹ Is this your son?
(talking to a man)

---

3   CAN I HAVE…

3 minutes

Ask if you can have these items in Arabic.

❶ coffee with milk   ❷ baklava   ❸ black coffee   ❹ Turkish delight

6 rice

7 cheese

knife 8

9 napkin

10 juice

At the table

6 رُز
ruz

7 جبنة
gibna

8 سكينة
sikkeena

9 فوطة
fooTa

10 عصير
Aaseer

---

4 RESTAURANT

4 minutes

You arrive at a restaurant. Join in the conversation, replying in Arabic following the numbered English prompts.

masaa il-kheir
❶ Hello. A table for six please.

tadkheen aw doon tadkheen?
❷ Non-smoking.

itfaDDaloo hina
❸ Can I have the menu, please?

Aawzeen mayya maAdaneyya?
❹ No. A tamarind drink, please.

HaaDir
❺ I don't have a wineglass.

Restaurant

❶ أهلاً. مائدة لستة، من فضلك.
ahlan. maa'ida li-sitta, min faDlak

❷ دون تدخين.
doon tadkheen

❸ ممكن المنيو, من فضلك؟
mumkin il-menu, min faDlak

❹ لا، تمر هندي، من فضلك.
laa. tamr hindi, min faDlak

❺ ماعنديش كاس.
ma Aandeesh kaas

1

WARM UP

1 minute

Say "**He is vegetarian**" (pp.14–15).

Say "**She is not from Egypt**" and "**I don't have a car**" (pp.14–15).

What is the Arabic for "**children**"? (pp.10–11).

Il-ayyaam wish-shuhoor
DAYS AND MONTHS

In Arabic, the word **yoom** (*day*) is sometimes used in front of the days of the week (**usbooA**), for example, **yoom il-itnein** (*Monday*). Note that in the Middle East, the weekend typically falls on Friday and Saturday, with offices and schools often opening again on Sunday.

2

WORDS TO REMEMBER: DAYS

5 minutes

الأثنين **il-itnein**	Monday	
التلات **ittalaat**	Tuesday	
الأربع **il-arbaA**	Wednesday	
الخميس **il-khamees**	Thursday	
الجمعة **il-gumAa**	Friday	
السبت **is-sabt**	Saturday	
الأحد **il-Had**	Sunday	
النهاردة **innahaarda**	today	
بكرة **bokra**	tomorrow	
إمبارح **embareH**	yesterday	

Familiarize yourself with these words, then test yourself using the cover flap.

عندي حجز للنهاردة.
Aandee Hagz lil-nahaarda
I have a reservation for today.

الاجتماع بكرة.
il-igtimaaA bokra
The meeting is tomorrow.

3

USEFUL PHRASES: DAYS

2 minutes

Learn these phrases, then test yourself using the cover flap.

الاجتماع مش يوم الثلاثاء. **il-igtimaaA mish yoom ittalaat**	The meeting isn't on Tuesday.	
باشتغل يوم الجمعة. **bashtaghal yoom il-gumAa**	I work on Fridays.	

4 WORDS TO REMEMBER: MONTHS

5 minutes

In Arabic, the months have fairly similar names to English. Familiarize yourself with these words, then test yourself using the cover flap.

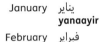

عيد زواجنا في يوليو.
Aeed zawaagna fi yoolyo
Our wedding anniversary is in July.

رمضان شهر الصوم.
ramaDaan shahr is-soom
Ramadan is the month of fasting.

January	يناير **yanaayir**
February	فبراير **febraayir**
March	مارس **maaris**
April	أبريل **abreel**
May	مايو **maayo**
June	يونيو **yoonyo**
July	يوليو **yoolyo**
August	أغسطس **aghusTus**
September	سبتمبر **sebtamber**
October	أكتوبر **octoobar**
November	نوفمبر **novamber**
December	ديسمبر **disamber**
month	شهر **shahr**
year	سنة **sana**

5 USEFUL PHRASES: MONTHS

2 minutes

Learn these phrases, then test yourself using the cover flap.

My children have a holiday in August.
أولادي عندهم اجازة في أغسطس.
awlaadee Aanduhum agaaza fi aghusTus

My birthday is in June.
عيد ميلادي في يونيو.
Aeed milaadee fi yoonyo

IssaaAa wil-arqaam
TIME AND NUMBERS

1 **WARM UP**

1 minute

Count in Arabic from
1 to 10 (pp.10–11).

Say "**I have a reservation**"
(pp.20–21).

Say "**The meeting is on
Wednesday**" (pp.28–9).

The word **saaAa** means *hour* or *watch*, and is used for telling the time: **issaaAa talaata** (literally *the hour three*); **issaaAa kaam?** (literally *the hour how many?* or *what's the time?*). In English, the minutes come first: *five to two*; in Arabic, the hour comes first: **itnein illa khamsa** (literally *two except five*). Twenty minutes is referred to as **tilt** (*a third*).

2 **WORDS TO REMEMBER:** TIME

4 minutes

Familiarize yourself with these words,
then test yourself using the cover flap.

الساعة واحدة **issaaAa waaHda**	one o'clock
واحدة وخمسة **waaHda we khamsa**	five past one
واحدة وربع **waaHda we rubA**	quarter past one
واحدة وثلث **waaHda we tilt**	twenty past one ["one and a third"]
واحدة ونص **waaHda we nuS**	half past one
اثنين إلا ربع **itnein illa rubA**	quarter to two
اثنين إلا عشرة **itnein illa Aashra**	ten to two

3 **USEFUL PHRASES**

2 minutes

Learn these phrases, then test yourself
using the cover flap.

الساعة كام؟ **issaaAa kaam**	What time is it?
عاوزين الفطار الساعة كام؟ **Aawzeen il-fiTaar issaaAa kaam**	What time do you want breakfast?
الاجتماع الساعة إتناشر. **il-igtimaaA issaaAa itnaashar**	The meeting is at 12 o'clock.

4 WORDS TO REMEMBER: HIGHER NUMBERS

6 minutes

In Arabic, for the numbers from 20 to 99, units are said before tens, and the numbers are linked with **wi** (and)—for example, 21 is **waaHid wi Aishreen** (literally *one and-twenty*), 36 is **sitta wi talateen** (*six-and-thirty*), 78 is **tamanya wi sabaAeen** (*eight-and-seventy*), and so on.

One thousand is **alf**, and the words for subsequent thousands build on the same basic term—for example, **settalaaf** (6,000). The dual ending **-ein** (pp.10–11), is used for 200 (**miyatein**) and 2,000 (**alfein**).

Familiarize yourself with these words, then test yourself using the cover flap.

دفعت خمسة وتمانين جنيه بكارت واي فاي.
dafaAt khamsa wetamaneed geneih becart waiy faiy
I've paid eighty-five pounds by contactless payment.

eleven	حداشر **Hidaashar**
twelve	إتناشار **itnaashar**
thirteen	ثلاثة عشر **talattaashar**
fourteen	أربعتاشر **arbAtaashar**
fifteen	خمستاشر **khamsataashar**
sixteen	ستاشر **sittaashar**
seventeen	سبعتاشر **sabaAtaashar**
eighteen	تمنتاشر **tamantaashar**
nineteen	تسعتاشر **tisaAtaashar**
twenty	عشرين **Aishreen**
thirty	ثلاثين **talaateen**
forty	أربعين **arbaAeen**
fifty	خمسين **khamseen**
sixty	ستين **sitteen**
seventy	سبعين **sabAeen**
eighty	ثمانين **tamaneen**
ninety	تسعين **tisAeen**
hundred	مية **meyya**
ten thousand	عشرتلاف **Aashartalaf**
one hundred thousand	ميت ألف **meet alf**
one million	مليون **miliyoon**

5 SAY IT

2 minutes

twenty-five
sixty-eight
eighty-four
ninety-one
five to ten
half past eleven
What time is lunch?

Il-mawaaeed
APPOINTMENTS

<table>
<tr><td>

1 WARM UP

1 minute

Say the days of the week in Arabic (pp.28–29).

Say **"It's three o'clock"** (pp.30–31).

What's the Arabic for **"today," "tomorrow,"** and **"yesterday"**? (pp.28–29).

</td><td>

Business in the Arabic-speaking world is generally conducted more formally than in Britain or the US; always address business contacts as **haᴅretak/ haᴅretek** (formal *you*). Traditional hospitality also extends to business situations. You may be offered drinks and snacks at meetings, and it is polite to accept. Offices don't close for lunch, and people often eat at their workplace or at street food stalls.

</td></tr>
</table>

2 USEFUL PHRASES

5 minutes

Learn these phrases, then test yourself using the cover flap.

نتقابل بكرة؟ **nit'aabil bokra**	Shall we meet tomorrow?
مع مين؟ **maᴀa meen**	With whom?
إنت فاضي امتى؟ **enta faaᴅi imta**	When are you free?
آسف، أنا مشغول. **aasif, ana mashghool**	Sorry, I am busy.
الخميس كويس؟ **il-khamees kwayyis**	Is Thursday OK?
أيوه ده يناسبني. **aywah, dah yinaasibnee**	That suits me.

أهلاً
ahlan
Welcome.

سلام باليد
salaam bil-yad
handshake

3 IN CONVERSATION

مساء الخير.
أنا عندي ميعاد.
**masaa il-kheir.
ana ᴀandee miᴀaad**

Good afternoon. I have an appointment.

ميعادك مع مين؟
miᴀaadak maᴀa meen

Who is your appointment with?

مع الأستاذ حسن.
maᴀa al-ustaaz Hasan

With Mr. Hassan.

4 PUT INTO PRACTICE

5 minutes

Complete this dialogue, then test yourself using the cover flap.

نتقابل الخميس؟
nit'aabil il-khamees

Shall we meet
on Thursday?

Say: Sorry, I'm busy.

آسف، أنا مشغول.
aasif, ana mashghool

يناسبك امتى؟
yinaasabak imta

When would suit you?

Say: Tuesday afternoon.

التلات بعد الظهر.
it-talaat baAd iD-Duhr

يناسبك الساعة أربعة؟
yenasbak essaAa arbaAa

Is four o'clock
good for you?

Say: Yes, that suits me.

أيوة مناسب.
aywah, munasib

Cultural tip If you are talking as a woman or to a
woman, you need to add the ending **-a** to descriptive
words such as **aasif** (sorry), **faaDi** (free), **mashghool**
(busy), and **mitakh-khar** (late). A woman would say:
aasfa, ana mashgoola (sorry, I'm busy) or **ana
mitakh-khara** (I'm late). You would ask a woman
enti faaDya? (are you free?).

---

4 minutes

الساعة كام ميعادك؟
issaaAa kaam miAaadak

What time is your
appointment?

الساعة ثلاثة، بس أنا متأخر.
**issaaAa talaata, bass
ana mit'akh-khar**

Three o'clock, but
I'm late.

مفيش مشكلة. اتفضل
استريح.
**mafeesh mushkila.
itfaDDal estarayyaH**

No problem. Please
take a seat.

1 WARM UP 🍰
1 minute

Say "**I'm sorry**" (pp.32–33).

What is the Arabic for
"**I have an appointment**"?
(pp.32–33).

How do you say "**when?**"
in Arabic? (pp.32–33).

Aalat-tilifoon
ON THE TELEPHONE

Emergency numbers for police, ambulance, and fire services vary by country, and it is best to look up the local numbers when you reach your destination. Public telephones are rare, so it is a good idea to buy a local SIM card for your cell phone. To make direct international calls from most MENA countries, dial the access code 00, then the country code, area code (omit the initial 0), and phone number.

2 🔊 MATCH AND REPEAT

Match the numbered items to the list,
then test yourself using the cover flap.

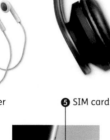

1 earbuds

❶ سماعات
sammaAaat

❷ سماعات رأس
sammaAaat raas

❸ cell phone

❸ موبايل
mubayil

❹ شاحن
shaaHin

❹ charger

❺ SIM card

❺ سيم كارت
sim-kart

❻ تليفون
tilifoon

❼ أنسر ماشين
ansar mahsheen

ممكن أشتري
سيم كارت محلي؟
**mumkin ashtari
sim-kart maHallee**
Can I buy a local SIM card?

3 🔊 IN CONVERSATION

آلو. معاك عزة بركات.
**aaloh. maAak Azza
barakaat**

Hello. Azza Barakat
speaking.

ممكن أكلم الأستاذ
بدران من فضلك؟
**mumkin akallim il-ustaaz
badraan, min faDlik**

Can I speak to
Mr. Badraan, please?

مين معايا؟
meen maAaya

Who's calling?

<table>
</table>

5 SAY IT
2 minutes

Can I speak to Mr. Hassan?

Can I buy a charger?

Can I leave a message for Yara?

I'll call him back on Wednesday.

4 minutes

❷ headphones

❻ telephone

answering machine ❼

---

4 🔊 USEFUL PHRASES
4 minutes

Learn these phrases, then test yourself using the cover flap.

ممكن رقم مازن؟
mumkin raqam Mazen

Can I have the number for Mazen?

ممكن أكلم رنا؟
mumkin akallem Rana

Can I speak to Rana?

ممكن أسيب رسالة؟
mumkin aseeb risaala

Can I leave a message?

أنا آسف. النمرة غلط.
ana aasif, in-nimra ghalaT

I'm sorry, wrong number.

---

4 minutes

هاري نولز من مطابع كابيتال.
haaree noolz min maTaabiA kabitaal

Harry Knowles from Capital Printers.

أنا آسفة. الخط مشغول.
ana aasfa. il-khaTT mashghool

I'm sorry. The line is busy.

هاتصل بعدين.
hattasil baAdein

I'll call back later.

RaagiA wi karrar
REVIEW AND REPEAT

Telephones

❶ موبايل
mubayil

❷ تليفون
tilifoon

❸ سماعات رأس
sammaAaat raas

❹ سيم كارت
sim-kart

---

1 **TELEPHONES**

Name these items in Arabic.

❶ cell phone
❷ telephone
headphones ❸

When?

❶ I have a meeting on Monday.

❷ My birthday is in September.

❸ Today is Friday.

❹ I work on Sundays.

---

2 **WHEN?**

2 minutes

What do these sentences mean?

❶ ana Aandee igtimaaA yoom il-itnein

❷ Aeed milaadee fi sebtembir

❸ innahaarda il-gumAa

❹ bashtaghal yoom il-Had

Time

❶ الساعة واحدة
issaaAa waaHda

❷ واحدة وخمسة
waaHda we khamsa

❸ واحدة وربع
waaHda we rubA

❹ واحدة وثلث
waaHda we tilt

❺ واحدة ونص
waaHda we nuS

❻ اثنين إلا عشرة
itnein illa Ashra

---

3 **TIME**

3 minutes

Say these times in Arabic.

❶　❷　❸

❹　❺　❻

3 minutes

4 **SUMS**

4 minutes

Say the answers to these sums in Arabic.

❶ 10 + 6 = ?

❷ 14 + 25 = ?

❸ 66 − 13 = ?

❹ 40 + 34 = ?

❺ 90 + 9 = ?

❻ 46 − 5 = ?

❹ SIM card

Sums

❶ ستاشر
sittaashar

❷ سبعة وثلاثين
sabAa wi-talateen

❸ ثلاثة وخمسين
talaata wi-khamseen

❹ أربعة وسبعين
arbaAa wi-sabaAeen

❺ تسعة وتسعين
tisAa watesAeen

❻ واحد وأربعين
waaHid warbeAeen

5 **I WANT...**

3 minutes

Fill in the blanks with the correct form of **Aawiz** (*want*).

❶ howwa _____ ahwa

❷ heyya _____ mayya

❸ eHna _____ Aaseer

❹ hum _____ shokolaata?

❺ enta _____ shaay?

❻ enti _____ eh?

I want...

❶ عاوز
Aawiz

❷ عاوزة
Aawza

❸ عاوزين
Aawzeen

❹ عاوزين
Aawzeen

❺ عاوز
Aawiz

❻ عاوزة
Aawza

Fi shibbaak it-tazaakir
AT THE TICKET OFFICE

1 WARM UP
1 minute

Count to 100 in tens (pp.10–11, pp.30–31).

Ask **"What time is it?"** (pp.30–31).

Say **"It's half past one"** (pp.30–31).

In MENA countries with a rail network, trains can be an economic alternative to planes. In Egypt, for instance, tourists can take a comfortable **aarabit noom** (*sleeper car*) from Cairo to Luxor or Aswan. Many large train stations will have ticket offices that take cash and cards. Some places may also accept mobile and digital payments.

2 WORDS TO REMEMBER

3 minutes

Familiarize yourself with these words, then test yourself using the cover flap.

رصيف **raSeef**	platform
قطار **'aTr**	train
تذكرة **tazkara**	ticket
ذهاب **dhahaab**	single
ذهاب وعودة **dhahaab w-Aawda**	return
درجة أولى **daraga oola**	first class
درجة ثانية **daraga tanya**	second class
محطة الأوتوبيس **maHaTTit il-otobees**	bus station

لوحة **looHa** — sign

محطة القطار **maHaTTit il-'aTr** — train station

المحطة زحمة. **il-maHaTTa zaHma** The station is crowded.

ركاب **rukkaab** passengers

3 IN CONVERSATION

تذكرتين للأقصر، من فضلك. **tazkartein li-lu'Sur, min faDlak**

Two tickets to Luxor, please.

ذهاب وعودة؟ **dhahaab w-Aawda**

Return?

أيوه. لازم نحجز كراسي؟ **aywah. laazim niHgiz karaasi**

Yes. Do we need to reserve seats?

4   USEFUL PHRASES

5 minutes

Learn these phrases, then test yourself using the cover flap.

القطار متأخر.
il-'aTr mitakh-khar
The train is late.

How much is a ticket to Aswan?	بكام التذكرة لأسوان؟ **bikaam it-tazkara l'aswaan**
Two tickets to Cairo, please.	تذكرتين للقاهرة، من فضلك. **tazkartein lil-qaahira, min fadlak**
Can I pay by card?	ممكن أدفع بالكارت؟ **mumkin adfaA bil-kart**
Do I have to change trains?	لازم أغير القطار؟ **laazim aghayyar il-'aTr**
Which platform does the train leave from?	من أي رصيف يغادر القطار؟ **min ay raSeef yughaadir il-'aTr**
Do we have to reserve seats?	لازم نحجز كراسي؟ **laazim niHgiz karaasi**
What time is the train for Alexandria?	قطار اسكندرية الساعة كام؟ **'aTr iskindereyya issaAaa kaam**

Conversational tip
The plural of **tazkara** (*ticket*) is **tazaakir**: **talat tazaakir l'aswaan** (*three tickets to Aswan*). *Two tickets* is **tazkartein**, an example of how the final **a** of **tazkara** changes to a **t** when the special dual ending **-ein** is added (pp.11–12).

5 SAY IT
2 minutes

What time is the train for Aswan?

How much is a ticket to Luxor?

Three return tickets to Giza, please.

4 minutes

أيوة. القطر هيغادر من رصيف نمرة خمسة.
aywah. il'aTr hayghaadir min raSeef nimra khamsa
Yes. The train leaves from platform five.

ممكن أدفع بالكارت؟
mumkin adfaA bil-kart
Can I pay by card?

ايوة. خمستلاف جنيه من فضلك.
aywah. khamastalaaf geneih min faDlik
Yes. Five thousand pounds, please.

RaayiH wi waakhid
TO GO AND TO TAKE

1 WARM UP
1 minute

How do you say **"train"** in Arabic? (pp.38–39).

What does **"bikaam it-tazkara l'aswaan?"** mean? (pp.38–39).

Ask a man and a woman **"When are you free?"** (pp.32–33).

RaayiH and **waakhid** mean *to go* and *to take*, and are placed directly after the subject, without the need for *am*, *is*, or *are*. As with **Aawiz** (*to want*), you will need to add **-a** for a woman and **-een** for a group: **howwa raayiH** (*he is going*); **ummee raayHa** (*my mother is going*); **humma hayakhdoo** (*they are taking*).

2 🔊 RAAYIH: TO GO
6 minutes

The pronoun isn't needed if the subject is clear, but make sure you're using the correct form of **raayiH** for a man, woman, or group: **raayiH/raayHa/raayHeen fein?** for *where are you going?* (masculine/feminine/plural). Practice **raayiH** (*to go*) and the sample sentences, then test yourself using the cover flap.

أنا رايح/رايحة **ana raayiH/raayHa**	I am going (m/f)
أنت رايح **enta raayiH**	you are going (m)
أنت رايحة **enti raayHa**	you are going (f)
هو رايح **howwa raayiH**	he is going
هي رايحة **heyya raayHa**	she is going
احنا رايحين **eHna raayHeen**	we are going
انتم رايحين **entum raayHeen**	you are going (pl)
همّا رايحين **humma raayHeen**	they are going

احنا مش رايحين الجيزة.
eHna mish raayHeen ig-geeza — We are not going to Giza.

أنا رايح الأقصر.
ana raayiH lu'sur — I'm (m) going to Luxor.

Conversational tip You may have noticed that when you add **-a** for a woman or **-een** for a group to **raayiH** (*to go*), **waakhid** (*to take*), and **Aawiz** (*to want*), the **i** sound disappears. While the words would technically become, for example, **raayiHa**, **waakhida**, and **Aawizeen**, in everyday speech the sounds are compressed to become **raayHa**, **waakhda**, and **Aawzeen**: **heyya raayHa ig-geeza** (*she's going to Giza*); **heyya waakhda taksi men il-qahira lil-giza** (*she takes a taxi from Cairo to Giza*); **humma Aawzeen tazkartein** (*they want two tickets*).

3   WAAKHID: TO TAKE

6 minutes

Practice **waakhid** (*to take*) and the sample sentences, then test yourself using the cover flap.

إحنا هناخد المترو النهاردة.
eHna hanakhud el-metro innahaarda
We're taking the metro today.

I am taking (m/f)	أنا هاخد **ana haakhud**
you are taking (m)	إنت هتاخد **enta hatakhud**
you are taking (f)	إنتي هتاخدي **enti hatakhdee**
he is taking	هو هياخد **howwa hayakhud**
she is taking	هي هتاخد **heyya hatakhud**
we are taking	إحنا هناخد **eHna hanakhud**
you are taking (pl)	إنتم هتاخدو **entum hatakhdoo**
they are taking	همة هياخدو **humma hayakhdoo**

He's not going to take a taxi.
هو مش هياخد تاكسي.
howwa mish hayakhud taaksi

Are you (pl) going to take the bus?
إنتم هتاخدوا الأتوبيس؟
entum hatakhdoo el-otobees

4   PUT INTO PRACTICE

2 minutes

Complete this dialogue, then test yourself using the cover flap.

رايح فين؟
raayiH fein
Where are you going?

أنا رايح الجيزة.
ana raayiH ig-geeza

Say: I'm going to Giza.

إنت هتاخد تاكسي؟
enta hatakhud taaksi
Are you going to take a taxi?

لا, أنا هاخد القطار.
laa, ana haakhud il-'aTr

Say: No, I'm going to take the train.

1 WARM UP
1 minute

Say "**I'm not taking a taxi**" (pp.40–41).

Ask a group of people "**Where are you going?**" (pp.40–41).

Say "**fruit**" and "**cheese**" (pp.22–23).

Taaksi, otobees, wi metro
TAXI, BUS, AND METRO

In Egypt you can hail a taxi, but in other MENA countries, you may need to go to a taxi stand. Ridesharing services are popular, and you may be able to get a shared taxi or **mekrobaas** (*microbus*) in Egypt. Egyptians generally use the word **otobees** for bus, but in other regions you might hear **baas** or **Haafila**. About a dozen cities in the Arab-speaking world also have a metro system.

2 🔊 WORDS TO REMEMBER
4 minutes

Familiarize yourself with these words, then test yourself using the cover flap.

أوتوبيس **otobees**	bus
محطة أتوبيسات **maHaTTit otobeesat**	bus station
موقف أوتوبيس **mawqaf otobees**	bus stop
شباك تذاكر **shibbaak tazaakir**	ticket office
موقف تاكسي **mawqaf taaksi**	taxi stand
أجرة تاكسي **ogrit taaksi**	taxi fare
محطة مترو **maHaTTit metro**	metro station

أتوبيس ١٧ بيقف هنا؟
otobees sabaAtaashar beyo'af hina
Does the number 17 bus stop here?

3 🔊 IN CONVERSATION: TAXI
2 minutes

خان الخليلي من فضلك.
khan il-khalilee min faDlak
Khan il-khalili, please.

ماشي. اتفضل.
maashi. itfaDDal
OK. Please get in.

ممكن أنزل هنا من فضلك؟
mumkin anzil hina min faDlak
Can I get out here, please?

4 USEFUL PHRASES

4 minutes

Learn these phrases, then test yourself using the cover flap.

I want a taxi to Karnak.
عاوز تاكسي للكرنك.
Aawiz taaksi lil-karnak

Please wait for me.
استناني من فضلك.
istannaanee min faDlak

How far is it?
المسافة قد إيه؟
il-masaafa adda eh

How do I get to the museum?
ازاي أوصل المتحف؟
izzay awSal il-matHaf

When is the next bus?
امتى الأوتوبيس الجاي؟
imta il-otobees ig-gaay

Cultural tip Cairo has a large metro system, with Line 1 (blue) and Line 2 (red) running north–south, and Line 3 (green) running east–west. The three lines are also identified by the names of their end stations. Further expansion is underway, with a monorail, LRT, and three new proposed metro lines.

6 SAY IT

2 minutes

Does the number 6 stop here?

Are you going to Khan il-khalili?

How do I get to the train station?

5 IN CONVERSATION: BUS

2 minutes

رايح عند المتحف؟
raayiH Aand il-matHaf

Are you going to the museum?

أيوه. خمسة جنيه من فضلك.
awyah. khamsa gineih min faDlik

Yes. Five pounds please.

قوللي لما نوصل.
ullee lama nowSal

Tell me when we arrive.

1 WARM UP

1 minute

Say "**I have...**" (pp.14–15).

Say "**my father,**" "**my sister,**" and "**my son**" (pp.10–11, pp.12–13).

Say "**I'm going to Luxor**" (pp.40–41).

AalaT-Tareeq
ON THE ROAD

While rental cars are available quite easily in the MENA region, it is more relaxing to hire a car with a driver. If you decide to drive yourself, try to stick to the daytime, be clear about the route, and learn to recognize your destination in Arabic script. Note that the region has a mix of free and toll highways, so check your route before you set off.

2 ◀)) MATCH AND REPEAT

Match the numbered items to the list, then test yourself using the cover flap.

1 شنطة
shanTa

2 بربريز
barabreez

3 شاحن
shaaHin

4 محطة شحن سيارات
maHaTTit shaHn sayyaraat

5 باب
baab

6 كاوتش
kawitsh

7 فانوس
fanoos

8 كابل الشحن
kabl esh-shaHn

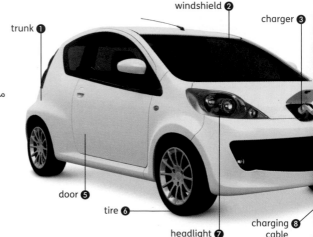

trunk **1**
windshield **2**
charger **3**
door **5**
tire **6**
headlight **7**
charging cable **8**

Cultural tip Gas pumps in Arabic-speaking countries are usually manned. The attendant will ask you how much fuel you need and fill the tank for you. You can pay by cash or card. Charging stations for electric cars may be found in big cities and along major highways and can be paid for by card or app.

3 ◀)) ROAD SIGNS

اتجاه واحد
ettegaah waaHid
One-way

دوران
dawaraan
Roundabout

ممنوع الدوران
mamnooA addawaraan
No U-turn

4 USEFUL PHRASES

4 minutes

Learn these phrases, then test yourself using the cover flap.

The blinker isn't working. الإشارة مش شغالة.
il-ishaara mish shagh-ghaala

Fill it up, please. فوّلها./املاها من فضلك.
fawwelha/imlaaha min faDlak

4 minutes

charging ❹ point/ station

5 WORDS TO REMEMBER

3 minutes

Familiarize yourself with these words, then test yourself using the cover flap.

car	عربية	**Aarabyya**
gas	بنزين	**banzeen**
diesel	ديزل	**deezil**
oil	زيت	**zeit**
engine	موتور	**motoor**
gearbox	فتيس	**fetees**
flat tire	عجلة نايمة	**Aagala nayma**
exhaust	عادم (سيارات)	**Aadem (sayyaraat)**
driving license	رخصة	**rukhsa**

6 SAY IT

1 minute

The headlights aren't working.

I don't have gas.

---

2 minutes

توقف
tawaqqaf
Stop

ممنوع الدخول
mamnooA eldokhool
No entry

ممنوع الوقوف
mamnooA alwoqoof
No parking

RaagiA wi karrar
REVIEW AND REPEAT

Transportation

❶ عربية
Aarabyya

❷ أوتوبيس
otobees

❸ تاكسي
taaksi

❹ درجة ثانية
daraga tanya

❺ مترو
metro

---

1 TRANSPORTATION

Name these forms of transportation in Arabic.

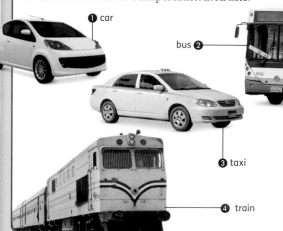

❶ car

bus ❷

❸ taxi

❹ train

Going/taking

❶ رايحة
raayHa

❷ رايحين
raayHeen

❸ رايح
raayiH

❹ هتاخدو
hatakhdoo

❺ هتاخد
hatakhud

❻ هتاخد
hatakhud

---

2 GOING/TAKING

4 minutes

Fill in the blanks with the correct form of
raayiH (*to go*) and **waakhid** (*to take*).

❶ enti _____ fein? (raayiH)

❷ humma _____ ig-geeza (raayiH)

❸ howwa _____ il-matHaf (raayiH)

❹ entum _____ il-metro? (waakhid)

❺ heyya mish _____ taaksi (waakhid)

❻ enta _____ il-otobees? (waakhid)

il-agweba *Answers*
(Cover with flap)

You?

① أنت عاوز عصير؟
enta Aawiz Aaseer

② أنت عندك ميعاد؟
enti Aandik meeAaad

③ أنتم من مصر؟
entum min maSr

④ أنت رايحة فين؟
enti raayHa fein

⑤ أنتم عندكم ملبن؟
entum Aandukum malban

---

3 minutes

⑤ metro

---

3 YOU?

4 minutes

Use the correct phrase for *you* (**enta, enti**, or **entum**) in each question.

① Ask a man "Do you want a juice?"

② Ask a woman "Do you have an appointment?"

③ Ask a group "Are you from Egypt?"

④ Ask a woman "Where are you going?"

⑤ Ask in a café "Do you have malban?"

---

4 TICKETS

4 minutes

You're buying tickets at a train station. Follow the conversation, replying in Arabic following the numbered English prompts.

sabaah il-kheir, ayy khidma?
① Two tickets to Aswan, please.

dhihaab wi-aawda?
② Yes. Return, please.

tisaeen gineih, min faDlak
③ What time is the train?

is-saaa khamsa we nuS
④ Do we have to reserve seats?

laa. mish muhimm
⑤ Thank you. Goodbye.

Tickets

① تذكرتين لأسوان، من فضلك.
tazkartein l'aswaan, min faDlik

② أيوه، ذهاب وعودة `.من فضلك
aywah. dhahaab w-Aawda, min faDlik

③ القطار الساعة كام؟
il-'aTr issaAaa kaam

④ لازم نحجز كراسي؟
laazim niHgiz karaasi

⑤ شكرا. مع السلامة.
shukran. maAasalaama

Hawl il-madeena
AROUND TOWN

1 **WARM UP**
1 minute

Ask "**How do you get to the museum?**" (pp.42–43).

Say "**I want to take the metro**" and "**I'm not taking a taxi**" (pp.40–41).

Egyptian Arabic may have some words in common with Modern Standard Arabic, but in many aspects, it is a distinct dialect. For example, in Egypt **kubree** is used widely for *bridge*, but **jisr** is common in other parts of the Arab world. Be careful, too, not to confuse similar sounding words like **maktaba** (*library/bookstore*) and **maktab** (*office*).

2 **WORDS TO REMEMBER**
4 minutes

Familiarize yourself with these words, then test yourself using the cover flap.

محطة بنزين **maнaттit banzeen**	gas station
مكتب سياحة **maktab siyaaнa**	tourist office
مكتبة **maktaba**	library/bookstore
وسط البلد **wesт il-balad**	town center

3 **MATCH AND REPEAT**
4 minutes

Match the numbered locations to the list, then test yourself using the cover flap.

❶ مسجد
masgid

❷ متحف
matнaf

❸ كوبري
kubree

❹ متحف فنون
matнaf fonoon

❺ ميدان
midaan

❻ برج
borg

❼ دار الأوبرا
daar il-obra

❽ سوق
soo'

❶ mosque

❷ museum

❸ bridge

❹ art gallery

opera house **❼**

tower **❻**

❺ square

4   USEFUL PHRASES

4 minutes

Learn these phrases, then test yourself using the cover flap.

Is there a gas station near here?	فيه محطة بنزين قريبة من هنا؟ **feeh maHaTTit banzeen urayyiba min hina**
(Is it) far from here?	بعيد من هنا؟ **biAeed min hina**
There is a market next to the bridge.	فيه سوق جنب الكوبري. **feeh soo' ganb il-kubree**
There isn't an art gallery.	مافيش متحف فنون. **ma feesh matHaf fonoon**

المسجد في وسط البلد.
il-masgid fi weST il-balad
The mosque is in the town center.

5   PUT INTO PRACTICE

2 minutes

Complete this dialogue, then test yourself using the cover flap.

فيه مكتبة قريبة من هنا؟
feeh maktaba urayyiba min hina

أي خدمة؟
ayyi khidma
Can I help you?

Ask: Is there a bookstore near here?

بعيد من هنا؟
biAeed min hina

أيوه، جنب المتحف.
aywah, ganb il-matHaf
Yes, next to the museum.

Ask: Is it far from here?

شكرا.
shukran

لا، هناك.
laa, hinaak
No, over there.

Say: Thank you.

❽ market

Conversational tip The common expressions **feeh** (there is/are) and **ma feesh** (there isn't/aren't) will be understood throughout the Arabic-speaking world, but in some dialects of Arabic **ma feesh** is pronounced **ma fee**, without the final **sh** sound. Likewise, **ma Aandeesh** (I don't have) and **ma Aandinaash** (we don't have) can be pronounced **ma Aandee** and **ma Aandinaa**, again without the final **sh** sound.

1 WARM UP
1 minute

Ask "**How far is it?**" (pp.42–43).

Say "**We're taking the bus**" (pp.40–41).

Ask a group of people "**Where are you going?**" (pp.40–41).

Il-ittigaahaat
DIRECTIONS

Finding your way around an unfamiliar town or city can be confusing, so it's a good idea to learn how to ask for and understand directions in Arabic. The smaller streets may not always be well known, so for easy navigation, it will be helpful to find out from residents what the local landmarks are, such as markets, shops, or important buildings.

2 WORDS TO REMEMBER

Familiarize yourself with these words, then test yourself using the cover flap.

إشارات المرور
ishaaraat elmoroor — traffic lights

شارع
shaareA — street

ناصية
nasya — corner

تقاطع
taqaatuA — intersection

خريطة
khareeTa — map

خرائط الإنترنت
kharayet al-internet — online maps

عمارة
Aimaara
apartment block

احنا فين؟
eHna fein
Where are we?

شارع رئيسي
shaareA ra'eesee
main street

3 IN CONVERSATION

فيه مطعم قريب؟
feeh maTAam uraayyib
Is there a restaurant nearby?

أيوه، جنب المحطة.
aywah. ganb il-maHaTTa
Yes, near the station.

ازاي أوصل المحطة؟
izzay awSal il-maHaTTa
How do I get to the station?

5 SAY IT
2 minutes

Turn right at the corner. (to a man)

Turn left in front of the museum. (to a woman)

How do I get to the restaurant?

4 USEFUL PHRASES
4 minutes

Learn these phrases, then test yourself using the cover flap.

turn left/right (to a man)	خذ شمال/يمين. **khud shimaal/yimeen**
turn left/right (to a woman)	خذي شمال/يمين. **khudee shimaal/yimeen**
first right	أول يمين **awwil yimeen**
second left	ثاني شمال **taanee shimaal**
straight on	على طول **Aala Tool**
the end of the street	آخر الشارع **aakhir ish-shaareA**
in front of	قدام **uddaam**
at	عند **Aand**
How do I get to the bazaar?	ازاي أوصل البازار؟ **izzay awsal il-bazaar**

تمثال
timsaal
statue

أنا تهت!
ana tuht
I'm lost!

---

4 minutes

خذي شمال عند الإشارة.
khudee shimaal Aand ishaaraat elmoroor
Turn left at the traffic lights.

المسافة قد إيه؟
il-misaafa adda eh
How far is it?

خمس دقائق مشي.
khamas da'aayi mashey
A five-minute walk.

1 WARM UP
1 minute

Say "**Is there a museum in town?**" (pp.48–49).

How do you say "**At six o'clock?**" (pp.30–31).

Ask "**What time is it?**" (pp.30–31).

Ziyaarit il-maAaalim
SIGHTSEEING

While many government offices are closed on Fridays, Saturdays, and public holidays, the main tourist sights are open through the week and often extend their hours during holidays; some are open late daily. Some shops, such as jewelry stores, may close on Sundays, but others remain open all week. Shops and sights remain open through prayer time.

2 ◁)) WORDS TO REMEMBER
4 minutes

Familiarize yourself with these words, then test yourself using the cover flap.

دليل سياحي **daleel siyaaHi**	guidebook, travel guide
مرشد سياحي **murshid syaaHee**	tour guide (m)
تذاكر دخول **tazaakir dukhool**	entrance tickets
دخول مجاني **dukhool maggaani**	free entrance
مواعيد الزيارة **mawaAeed iz-ziyaara**	opening times
أجازة رسمية **agaaza rasmeyya**	public holiday

جولة مع مرشدة
gawla maAa murshida
guided tour

Cultural tip Students get reduced admission rates at tourist sites. Once you enter, you may be offered the services of a guide—sometimes this is optional, but sometimes a guided tour is part of the ticket.

3 ◁)) IN CONVERSATION

بتفتحوا بعد الظهر؟
bi-tiftaHoo baAd iD-Duhr

Do you open in the afternoon?

أيوه، بس بنقفل الساعة خمسة.
aywah, bass bi-ni'fil issaaAa khamsa

Yes, but we close at five o'clock.

في أماكن لدخول كراسي بعجل؟
feeh amaaken ledokhool karaasee beAagal

Do you have wheelchair access?

4 USEFUL PHRASES

3 minutes

Learn these phrases, then test yourself using the cover flap.

What time do you open/close?

بتفتحوا/بتقفلوا الساعة كام؟
bi-tiftaHoo/bi-ti'filoo issaaAa kaam

Where are the restrooms?

فين الحمامات؟
fein il-Hammaamaat

Is there wheelchair access?

في أماكن لدخول كراسي بعجل؟
feeh amaaken ledokhool karaasee beAagal

5 PUT INTO PRACTICE

4 minutes

Complete this dialogue, then test yourself using the cover flap.

آسف، المتحف مقفول.
aasif. il-matHaf ma'fool

Sorry. The museum is closed.

Ask: Do you open on Tuesdays?

بتفتحوا يوم الثلاثاء؟
bi-tiftaHoo yoom it-talaat

أيوه، بس بنقفل بدري.
aywah, bass bi-ni'fil badree

Yes, but we close early.

Ask: At what time?

الساعة كام؟
issaaAa kaam

3 minutes

أيوه، فيه أسانسير.
aywah, feeh asanseir hinaak

Yes, there's an elevator over there.

شكرا. عاوزة تذكرتين دخول.
shukran. Aawza tazkartein dukhool

Thank you. I want two entrance tickets.

اتفضلي. الدليل السياحي ده مجاني.
ittfaDDalee. id-daleel is-siyaaHi dah maggaani

Here you are. This guidebook is free.

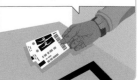

1 WARM UP
1 minute

Say in Arabic "**This is my father-in-law**" (pp.12–13).

What's the Arabic for "**ticket**" (pp.38–39).

Say "**I am going to Aswan**" (pp.40–41).

Fil-maTaar
AT THE AIRPORT

Although the airport environment is largely international, it is sometimes useful to be able to ask your way around the terminal in Arabic. It's always a good idea to make sure you have some small change when you arrive at the airport—you may need to pay for a luggage trolley or tip a porter.

2 WORDS TO REMEMBER
4 minutes

Familiarize yourself with these words, then test yourself using the cover flap.

تسجيل الوصول **tasgeel al-wusool**	check-in
مغادرة **mughaadra**	departures
وصول **wusool**	arrivals
جمارك **gamaarik**	customs
نقطة الجوازات **noqtat al-gawazaat**	passport control
صالة **saala**	terminal
بوابة **bawwaaba**	boarding gate
رحلة **riHla**	flight

رحلة تلاتة وعشرين هتغادر من صالة اثنين
riHla talata we Aeshreen hatghader men Saala itnein
Flight 23 leaves from Terminal 2.

3 USEFUL PHRASES
3 minutes

Learn these phrases, then test yourself using the cover flap.

رحلة أسوان في ميعادها؟
riHlit aswaan fi miAaad-ha
Is the flight to Aswan on time?

رحلة لندن متأخرة.
riHlit landan met'akhara
The flight to London is delayed.

مش لاقي شنطي.
mish laa'ee shonaTee
I can't find my luggage.

4 PUT INTO PRACTICE

3 minutes

Complete this dialogue, then test yourself using the cover flap.

أي خدمة؟
ayyi khidma

Can I help you?

Ask: Is the flight to
Hurghada on time?

رحلة الغردقة في ميعادها؟
**riHlit il-gharda'a fi
miAaad-ha**

أيوه يا فندم.
aywah yaa fandim

Yes, sir.

Ask: Which gate does
the flight leave from?

الرحلة من أي بوابة؟
**ir-riHla min ayyi
bawwaaba**

5 MATCH AND REPEAT

4 minutes

baggage check-in ❶   carry-on luggage ❷

passport ❸   ❹ boarding
pass

ticket ❺

❻ suitcase

❼ trolley

Match the numbered items
to the list, then test yourself
using the cover flap.

❶ تسجيل الشنط
tasgeel elshonaT

❷ شنطة يد
shanTat yad

❸ جواز السفر
gawaaz is-safar

❹ كارت صعود
kart suAood

❺ تذكرة
tazkara

❻ شنطة
shanTa

❼ تروللي
trollee

RaagiA wi karrar
REVIEW AND REPEAT

il-agweba *Answers*
(Cover with flap)

Places

❶ مسجد
masgid

❷ سوق
soo'

❸ متحف
matHaf

❹ متحف فنون
matHaf fonoon

❺ برج
borg

❻ كوبري
kubree

❼ ميدان
midaan

❽ دار الأوبرا
daar il-obra

---

il-agweba *Answers*
(Cover with flap)

1 PLACES

4 minutes

Name these locations in Arabic.

❶ mosque

❷ market

❸ museum

❹ art gallery

tower **❺**   bridge **❻**

❼ square   **❽** opera house

Car parts

❶ بربريز
barabreez

❷ شاحن
shaaHin

❸ محطة شحن سيارات
maHaTTit shaHn
sayyaraat

❹ باب
baab

❺ عجلة
Aagala

❻ كابل الشحن
kabl esh-shaHn

2 CAR PARTS

Name these car parts in Arabic.

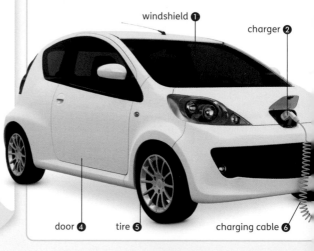

windshield **❶**   charger **❷**

door **❹**   tire **❺**   charging cable **❻**

3 QUESTIONS

4 minutes

Ask the questions in Arabic that match these answers.

❶ ana raayiH il-ahraam

❷ bi-ni'fil issaaAa arbaAa

❸ eHna Aawzeen shaay

❹ laa. mAandeesh awlaad

❺ khamas da'aayi mashey

Questions

❶ (أنت) رايح فين؟
(enta) raayiH fein

❷ بتقفلوا الساعة كام؟
bi-ti'filoo issaaAa kaam

❸ (أنتم) عاوزين إيه؟
(entum) Aawzeen eh

❹ عندك أولاد؟
Aandak awlaad

❺ المسافة قد إيه؟
il-misaafa adda eh

3 minutes

❸ charging point/ station

4 VERBS

4 minutes

Ask how to get to these places in Arabic.

❶ the museum

❷ the tower

❸ the market

❹ the mosque

❺ the bazaar

Verbs

❶ إزاي أوصل المتحف؟
izzay awsal il-matHaf

❷ إزاي أوصل البرج؟
izzay awsal il-borg

❸ إزاي أوصل السوق؟
izzay awsal is-soo'

❹ إزاي أوصل المسجد؟
izzay awsal il-masgid

❺ إزاي أوصل البازار؟
izzay awsal il-bazaar

1 WARM UP
1 minute

Ask **"Can I pay by card?"** (pp.38–39).

Ask **"How much is that?"** (pp.18–19).

Ask **"Do you have any children?"** (to a woman) (pp.10–11).

Hagz ghurfa
BOOKING A ROOM

A range of accommodations are available across the MENA region: **fundu'**, hotels usually rated one to five stars (pp.60–61); cheap and basic hostels; "floating hotels" in Nile cruisers; unique boutique hotels set in Moroccan riads, Berber villages, and Arab fortresses; and luxurious glamping sites. Airbnb, offering accommodation in private rooms and homes, is also a popular option.

2 USEFUL PHRASES
3 minutes

Learn these phrases, then test yourself using the cover flap.

شامل الفطور؟
shaamil il-fuToor
Is breakfast included?

فيه تكييف؟
feeh takyeef
Is there air-conditioning?

فيه خدمة غرف؟
feeh khidmit ghuraf
Is there room service?

المغادرة الساعة كام؟
il-mughaadra issaaAa kaam
What time is check-out?

3 IN CONVERSATION

فيه غرف فاضية؟
feeh ghuraf faDya
Do you have any rooms available?

أيوه، فيه غرفة لشخصين؟
aywah. feeh ghurfa li-shakhsein
Yes, there's a double room.

فيه سرير أطفال؟
feeh sireer aTfaal
Is there a cot?

4 WORDS TO REMEMBER

4 minutes

Familiarize yourself with these words, then test yourself using the cover flap.

فيه بلكونة؟
feeh balkoona
Is there a balcony?

room	غرفة	**ghurfa**
single room	غرفة لشخص	**ghurfa li-shakhS**
double room	غرفة لشخصين	**ghurfa li-shakhSein**
twin room	غرفة مزدوجة	**ghurfa muzdawaga**
bathroom	حمام	**Hammaam**
shower	دش	**dush**
balcony	بلكونة	**balkoona**
key	مفتاح	**moftaaH**
air-conditioning	تكييف	**takyeef**
breakfast	فطور	**fuToor**

5 SAY IT

2 minutes

Do you have a single room, please?

Six nights.

Is dinner included?

Cultural tip Most hotels in the MENA region will offer room rates with or without breakfast included. Breakfast is often in the style of a buffet, offering both international and local dishes. In Egypt, for instance, it usually includes a mix of Continental dishes such as juice, cereal, croissants, butter, and jam and Egyptian dishes such as **fool**, **falafel**, and **taAmyya**, alongside a choice of tea or coffee.

5 minutes

أيوه، فيه. عاوزين كام ليلة؟
aywah, feeh. Aawzeen kaam leila
Yes, there is. How many nights do you want?

ثلاث ليالي.
talat layaalee
Three nights.

تحت أمركم. اتفضلوا المفتاح.
taHt Amrukum. itfaDDaloo il-moftaaH
Of course. Here's the key.

1 WARM UP

1 minute

Ask "**Is/Are there...?**" and reply "**There isn't/ aren't...**" (pp.48–49).

What does "**ayyi khidma?**" mean (pp.48–49)?

Say "**They don't have any children**" (pp.14–15).

Fil-fundu'
IN THE HOTEL

Although the larger hotels always have bathrooms en suite, there are smaller hotels and guesthouses where you may have to share the facilities with other guests. The smaller hotels can have as few as 16 double or triple rooms and can be a low-cost option. The smallest guesthouses, known as **lukanda**, might not be very comfortable.

2 MATCH AND REPEAT

6 minutes

Match the numbered items to the list, then test yourself using the cover flap.

1 ستاير
sataayir

2 خدادية
khudadyya

3 نور
noor

4 تليفزيون
tilifizyoon

5 فوطة
fooTa

6 مخدة
makhadda

7 كرسي
kursee

8 سرير
sireer

9 روب حمام
roob Hammaam

10 شبشب
shibshib

11 بطانية
baTTanyya

1 curtains   **2** cushion   **3** light
4 television   towel **5**   **6** pillow
7 chair   bed **8**   bathrobe **9**
10 slippers   **11** blanket

Cultural tip In a double room in an Egyptian hotel, you may find one long pillow instead of two individual ones on the bed, though you can usually find regular rectangular pillows in the wardrobe. Do not hesitate to ask if you can't find any. You may also see an arrow on the floor or on a piece of furniture. This points toward Mecca, the direction Muslims face to pray. Toilets usually include a bidet spray, either hand-held or in the bowl, with an accessible tap to control the flow.

3 🔊 USEFUL PHRASES
5 minutes

Learn these phrases, then test yourself using the cover flap.

The room is very cold/hot.
الغرفة برد/حر جدا.
il-ghurfa bard/ Harr giddan

There are no towels.
مافيش فوط.
ma feesh fuwaT

We need some soap.
عاوزين صابون.
Aawzeen Saboon

The shower doesn't work.
الدش مش شغال.
id-dush mish shagh-ghaal

The elevator is out of order.
الأسانسير عطلان.
il-asanseir AaTlaan

4 🔊 PUT INTO PRACTICE
3 minutes

Complete this dialogue, then test yourself using the cover flap.

أي خدمة؟ عاوزة مخدة.
ayyi khidma Aawza makhadda
Can I help you?
Say: I need a pillow.

حابعتها حالا. والتليفزيون عطلان.
habAat-ha Haalan wal-tilifizyoon AaTlaan
I'll send one right away.
Say: And the television is out of order.

Aalal-markib
ON THE BOAT

Boat trips of all kinds are popular with visitors and travelers in the Middle East, whether a diving or snorkeling excursion in the Red Sea, a serene and spectacular sail down the Nile in a traditional felucca, or a luxurious sightseeing cruise in a "floating hotel."

2 **USEFUL PHRASES**

Learn these phrases, then test yourself using the cover flap.

ممكن عدة غوص؟
mumkin Aiddit ghaTs
Can we rent diving equipment?

أنا مبتدئ.
ana mubtadi'
I'm a beginner.

ماعرفش أعوم.
maAarafsh aAoom
I can't swim.

أنا سباح ماهر.
ana sabbaaH maahir
I'm an experienced swimmer.

الصيد مسموح هنا؟
is-seid masmooH hina
Is fishing allowed here?

دي مناسبة للأطفال؟
dee munaasba lil-aTfaal
Is it suitable for children?

ممكن نأجر مركب؟
mumkin niaggar markib
Can we rent a boat?

معدية
meAadeyya
ferry

3 **IN CONVERSATION**

عاوزين نحجز رحلة على النيل.
Aawzeen niHgiz riHla Aalan-neel

We want to book a cruise on the Nile.

أنا عندي أحسن فلوكة في النيل كله.
ana Aandee aHsan filooka fin-neel kulluh

I have the best felucca on the whole Nile.

ماشي. الرحلة كام ساعة؟
maashi. ir-riHla kaam saaAa

Okay. How many hours is the trip?

5 SAY IT

2 minutes

Can we rent diving gear?

I need a fishing rod.

How much is the trip for children?

---

3 minutes

شراع
shiraaA
sail

مركب شراعي
markib sheraaAee
sailboat/felucca

---

4 🔊 WORDS TO REMEMBER

4 minutes

Familiarize yourself with these words and phrases, then test yourself using the cover flap.

small boat	قارب	**'aareb**
sailboat/felucca	مركب شراعي	**markib sheraaAee**
motorboat/launch	لنش	**lansh**
yacht	يخت	**yakht**
dive boat	مركب غطس	**markib ghaTs**
diving gear	عدة الغطس	**Aiddit ghaTs**
snorkeling gear	عدة سنوركلنج	**Aiddit snurkeling**
fishing boat	مركب صيد	**markib seid**
fishing gear	عدة صيد	**Aiddit seid**
fishing rod	سنارة	**sinnaara**
bait	طعم	**TuAm**
life jacket	سترة النجاة	**sutrit in-nagaah**

---

5 minutes

ممكن ساعتين أو ثلاث ساعات.
mumkin saaAtein aw talaat saaAaat

It can be two or three hours.

بكام الرحلة دي لشخصين؟
bikaam ir-riHla dee li-shakhsein

How much is this trip for two people?

مية وخمسين جنيه النفر.
meyya wekhamseen gineih in-nafar

150 pounds per person.

Il-wasf
DESCRIPTIONS

1 WARM UP
1 minute

How do you say
"the room is hot?"
(pp.60–61).

What is the Arabic
for **"bed," "towel,"**
and **"pillow"**? (pp.60–61).

Adjectives are words used to describe people, things, and places, and can be used to easily make simple descriptive sentences. In Arabic, you generally put the adjective after the thing it describes and in the same gender and number—for example, **sireer kibeer** (*a large bed*, masculine/singular) or **ghurfa kibeera** (*a large room*, feminine/singular).

2 WORDS TO REMEMBER
7 minutes

Most adjectives change depending on whether the thing described is masculine or feminine. Generally, the feminine form of an adjective ends in **-a**. Be aware that this addition sometimes affects the pronunciation; the preceding vowel sounds may be contracted. Familiarize yourself with these words, then test yourself using the cover flap.

كبير/-ة	big/large	
kibeer/kibeera		
صغير/-ة	small	
sughayyar/sughayyara		
سخن/-ة	hot	
sukhn/sukhna		
بارد/-ة	cold	
baarid/baarda		
كويس/-ة	good/nice	
kwayyis/kwayyisa		
وحش/-ة	bad	
weHesh/weHsha		
بطيء/-ة	slow	
baTee'/baTee'a		
سريع/-ة	fast	
sareeA/sareeAa		
دوشة	noisy	
dawsha (m/f)		
هادي/-ة	quiet	
haadee/haadya		
قاسي/-ة	hard	
qaasee/qaaseya		
طري/-ة	soft	
Tari/Tariyya		
جميل/-ة	beautiful	
gameel/gameela		
وحش/-ة	ugly	
wehesh/wehsha		

الشجرة قديمة.
ish-shagara adeema
The tree is old.

الشمسيات جديدة.
ish-shamseyyat gideeda
The umbrellas are new.

الجو كويس.
ig-gaw kwayyis
The weather is nice.

3 USEFUL PHRASES

4 minutes

You can qualify a description by using **giddan** (*very*) or **shwayya** (*a little*) after the adjective. Learn these phrases, then test yourself using the cover flap.

The coffee is very hot.

القهوة سخن جدا.
il-ahwa sukhna giddan

My room is very noisy.

غرفتي دوشة جدا.
ghurfitee dawsha giddan

The car is a little small.

لعربية صغيرة شوية.
is-Aarabyya sughayyara shwayya

My pillow is a little hard.

مخدتي ناشفة شوية.
makhaddetee nashfa shwayya

4 PUT INTO PRACTICE

3 minutes

Complete this dialogue, then test yourself using the cover flap.

المنظر جميل جدا.
il-manzar gameel giddan

دي غرفتكم.
dee ghurfitkum
This is your room.

Say: The view is very beautiful.

ده صغير شوية.
dah sughayyar shwayya

الحمام هناك.
il-Hammaam hinaak
The bathroom is over there.

Say: It's a little small.

طيب، هناخد الغرفة دي.
Tayyeb, hanakhud elghorfa de

أنا آسف، مفيش أي غرف تانية.
ana aasif, mafeesh ay ghoraf tanya
I'm sorry, we don't have any other rooms.

Say: Then we'll take this room.

il-agweba *Answers*
(Cover with flap)

Adjectives

1 باردة
baarda

2 كبير
kibeer

3 سخنة
sukhna

4 جميل
gameel

5 هادية
haadya

In the hotel

1 تليفزيون
tilifizyoon

2 ستاير
sataayir

3 فوطة
fooTa

4 مخدة
makhadda

5 نور
noor

6 كرسي
kursee

7 شبشب
shibshib

8 سرير
sireer

9 روب حمام
roob Hammaam

RaagiA wi karrar
REVIEW AND REPEAT

1 ADJECTIVES

3 minutes

Fill in the blanks with the correct Arabic masculine or feminine form of the adjective given in brackets.

1 il-ghurfa _____ . (cold)

2 il Hammaam _____ giddan. (large)

3 il-mayya _____ shwayya. (hot)

4 il-baHr _____ . (beautiful)

5 ana Aawiz ghurfa _____ . (quiet)

2 IN THE HOTEL

Name these hotel room items in Arabic.

1 television **2** curtains **3** towel pillow **4**

6 chair **7** slippers bed **8** bathrobe **9**

il-agweba *Answers*
(Cover with flap)

3 AT THE HOTEL

4 minutes

You are booking a room in a hotel. Join in the conversation, replying in Arabic following the numbered English prompts.

ayyi khidma?
❶ Do you have any rooms available?

feeh ghurfa li-shakhs
❷ Is there air-conditioning?

aywah. ʌawiz kaam leila?
❸ Three nights.

maashi
❹ Is breakfast included?

taHt ʌmrukum. itfaDDaloo il-moftaaH
❺ Thank you very much.

At the hotel

❶ فيه غرف فاضية؟
feeh ghuraf faDya

❷ فيه تكييف؟
feeh takyeef

❸ ثلاث ليالي.
talat leyaalee

❹ شامل الفطور؟
shaamil il-fuToor

❺ شكرًا جزيلاً
shukran gazeelan

---

3 minutes

❺ light

---

4 NEGATIVES

5 minutes

Make these sentences negative using **mish** (*not*).

❶ il-ghurfa haadya

❷ il-ahwa sukhna

❸ eHna min maSr

❹ il-maTAam ganb il-maHaTTa

❺ howwa ʌawiz makhadda gideeda

Negatives

❶ الغرفة مش هادية.
il-ghurfa mish haadya

❷ القهوة مش سخنة.
il-ahwa mish sukhna

❸ احنا مش من مصر.
eHna mish min maSr

❹ المطعم مش جنب المحطة.
il-maTAam mish ganb il-maHaTTa

❺ هو مش عاوز مخدة جديدة.
howwa mish ʌawiz makhadda gideeda

Il-maHallaat
SHOPS

1 WARM UP
1 minute

Ask **"How do I get to the station?"** (pp.50–51).

Say **"Turn left at the traffic lights"** and **"The station is near the museum"** (pp.50–51).

Small, traditional, specialized shops and stalls are still common in Middle Eastern towns and cities, although you will also see chains and supermarkets within bigger cities and large shopping centers and malls on the outskirts. Markets and street vendors selling fresh local produce (and sometimes drinks and snacks) can be found everywhere.

2 MATCH AND REPEAT

Match the numbered shops to the list, then test yourself using the cover flap.

❶ مخبز
makhbaz

❷ حلواني
Halawaanee

❸ عطار
Attar

❹ جزار
gazzaar

❺ محل عصير
maHal Aaseer

❻ مكتبة
maktaba

❼ محل سمك
maHal samak

❽ جواهرجي
gawahirgee

❾ بنك
bank

❶ bakery

❷ pastry shop

❹ butcher

❺ juice bar

❼ fishmonger

❽ jeweler

Cultural tip A common sight on the streets of Cairo is the **makwagee** (*ironing shop*). For a small cost, you can have all your ironing done and delivered to you within a few hours. Other shops and services often available include the **maHaal gulood** (*leather shop*), which does shoe repairs, and the **labbaan** (*milkman*), who sells and delivers fresh milk, yogurt, and milk-based puddings.

محل الورد فين؟
maHaal il-ward fein
Where is the florist?

3 ◀)) USEFUL PHRASES

3 minutes

Learn these phrases, then test yourself using the cover flap.

Where is the hairdresser?	الكوافير فين؟	**il-kwaafeer fein**
Where do I pay?	أدفع فين؟	**adfaA fein**
I'm just looking, thank you.	بأخذ فكرة بس، شكرا.	**bakhud fikra bass, shukran**
Do you sell SIM cards?	بتبيعوا سيم كارت؟	**bitbeeAoo sim-kart**
May I have two of those?	ممكن اثنين من دول؟	**mumkin itnein min dool**
Can you order that for me?	ممكن تجهزلي طلبي؟	**mumkin tigahhizlee Talabee**

5 minutes

❸ spice shop

❻ bookshop

❾ bank

4 ◀)) WORDS TO REMEMBER

4 minutes

Familiarize yourself with these words, then test yourself using the cover flap.

antique shop	محل انتيكات	**maHal anteekaat**
hairdresser (women's)	كوافير	**kwaafeer**
post office	مكتب البريد	**maktab il-bareed**
shoe store	محل جزم	**maHal gizam**
dry cleaner	محل تنظيف	**maHal tanDeef**
grocer	بقال	**ba'aal**
produce store	خضري	**khudaree**
pharmacy	صيدلية	**saydaleyya**

5 SAY IT

2 minutes

Where is the bank?

Do you sell cheese?

May I have five of those?

Fil-bazaar
IN THE BAZAAR

Shopping in the traditional bazaars of the Arabic-speaking world is an experience not to be missed. As well as the usual tourist souvenirs and antiques, bazaars often have areas dedicated to particular local crafts or products, such as perfumes, spices, rugs, clothing, jewelry, leather, and furniture, as well as fresh produce and cooked foods. It is almost always possible to bargain at bazaars.

1 | WARM UP
1 minute

What is Arabic for "**40**," "**56**," "**77**," "**82**," and "**94**"? (pp.10–11, pp.30–31).

Say "**I need a big room**" (pp.64–65).

Ask "**Do you have a small car?**" (pp.58–59, pp.64–65).

2 | MATCH AND REPEAT

Match the numbered items to the list, then test yourself using the cover flap.

❶ جلابية
galabeyya

❷ طبق نحاس محفور
Taba' nehaas maHfoor

❸ فانوس
fanoos

❹ قنديل
qandeel

❺ شيشة
sheesha

❻ زير
zeer

❼ أبريق
Abreeq

❽ تمثال
timsaal

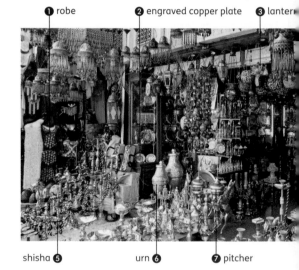

❶ robe ❷ engraved copper plate ❸ lantern

shisha ❺   urn ❻   ❼ pitcher

3 | IN CONVERSATION

عاوزة جلابية قطن
Aawza galabeyya uTn
I want a cotton robe.

عندي دي. جميلة!
Aandee dee. gameela
I have this one. Beautiful!

أيوه، جميلة. بكام دي؟
aywah, gameela. bi-kaam dee
Yes, it's beautiful. How much is it?

5 SAY IT
1 minute

I want a silk robe.

Do you have papyrus?

One hundred and ninety is fair.

That's expensive.

---

4 minutes

❹ chandelier

❽ statue

---

4 🔊 USEFUL PHRASES
4 minutes

Learn these phrases, then test yourself using the cover flap.

أي خدمة ثانية يا مدام؟
ayyi khidma tanya yaa madaam

Anything else, madam?

دي غالية جدا.
dee ghalya giddan

That's very expensive.

ده آخر كلام؟
dah aakhir kalaam

Is that your final price?

Cultural tip Bargaining is an essential part of the shopping experience in a bazaar. Stall holders expect you to haggle, but it is better to keep the negotiation light-hearted rather than turning it into a battle of wills. Remember that you will always strike a better bargain if you are prepared to buy more than one item from the same stall.

---

5 minutes

ميتين جنيه بس.
metein gineih bass

Only 200 pounds.

لا، دي غالية. مية وخمسين كويس.
laa, dee ghalya. mia wi-khaseen kwayyis

No, that's expensive. 150 is fair.

ماشي. مية وسبعين علشانك انت بس.
maashi. meyya wi-sabaAeen Aalashaanik enti bass

OK. 170 just for you.

1 WARM UP
1 minute

What are these items
you could buy in a
supermarket? (pp.22–23).

samak
gibna
makarona
laHma
khuDaar
firaakh

Fil-subermarkit
AT THE SUPERMARKET

Until recently, self-service shopping was not very
common in the Arabic-speaking world. However,
with more supermarkets now appearing in the
larger towns and resorts, the system is becoming
increasingly widespread. Supermarkets offer a
wide range of products, including groceries, fresh
produce, and packaged goods. They also often
have their own in-house bakery, butcher, and
cheese counter, and may serve takeout meals.

2 MATCH AND REPEAT
5 minutes

Match the numbered items to the list, then test
yourself using the cover flap.

❶ منتجات منزلية
muntagaat manzileyya

❷ منتجات تجميل
muntagaat tagmeel

❸ فواكه
fawaakih

❹ مشروبات
mashroobaat

❺ وجبات جاهزة
wagbaat gahza

❻ خضار
khuDaar

❼ منتجات مجمدة
muntagaat mugammada

❽ منتجات ألبان
muntagaat albaan

household products ❶
beauty products ❷
fruit ❸
drinks ❹
ready meals ❺
vegetables ❻
frozen foods ❼
dairy products ❽

Cultural tip The Arabic words for everyday items and basic
foods can vary depending on the dialect of the region. For
example, in Egypt milk is generally called **laban** and bread is
called **Aeish**, but in some other parts of the Arabic-speaking
world, the words **Haleeb** and **khubz** are more common.

3 USEFUL PHRASES

 3 minutes

Learn these phrases, then test yourself using the cover flap.

I already have a bag, thank you.	معايا شنطة تانية، شكرًا. **maAaya shanTa tanya, shukran**
Where are the drinks?	المشروبات فين؟ **il-mashroobaat fein**
Where do I pay?	أدفع فين؟ **adfaA fein**
Please type in your PIN.	اكتب الرقم السري من فضلك. **ekteb erraqam esserry min faDlak**

4 WORDS TO REMEMBER

 4 minutes

Familiarize yourself with these words, then test yourself using the cover flap.

milk	لبن **laban**
bread	عيش **Aeish**
butter	زبدة **zibda**
salt	ملح **malH**
pepper	فلفل **filfil**
laundry detergent	مسحوق غسيل **masHoo' ghaseel**
dish soap	مسحوق أطباق **masHoo' aTbaa'**
toilet paper	ورق تواليت **wara' twaalett**
hand sanitizer	معقم إيدين **muAaqqem edeen**

5 SAY IT

2 minutes

Where are the dairy products?

May I have some chicken, please?

Where are the frozen foods?

1 WARM UP
1 minute

Ask **"Can I have...?"** (pp.24–25).

Ask **"Do you have...?"** (pp.12–13).

Say "**38**," "**42**," and "**46**" (pp.10–11, pp.30–31).

Say "**big**" and "**small**" (pp.64–65).

Il-malaabis wil-gizam
CLOTHES AND SHOES

Clothes and shoes are measured in metric sizes—clothes size is **ma'aas elhodoom** and shoe size is **ma'aas elgazma**. Women's clothing is described as **Hareemee**, from the old word **Hareem** (*women*). You can negotiate prices in smaller, nonbrand stores but not in malls or bigger stores. You can also have custom items tailored at a reasonable price.

2 MATCH AND REPEAT

Match the numbered items to the list, then test yourself using the cover flap.

1 قميص
amees

2 كرافتة
kravatta

3 كم
komm

4 جاكيت
jaket

5 جيب
geib

6 بنطلون
banTaloon

7 جزمة
gazma

shirt **1**
tie **2**
sleeve **3**
pocket **5**
pants **6**
shoes **7**

Cultural tip Words for Western clothing vary between regions: **jeeba** (*skirt*) can also be **gunella** or **tannoora**. Traditional garments vary in style and have different names in different areas. Such items include the Egyptian **galabeyya** robe, the Palestinian **kufeyya** scarf, and the long, white **dishdasha** or **thawb** worn in the Gulf.

3 USEFUL PHRASES

5 minutes

Learn these phrases, then test yourself using the cover flap.

Is there a larger size?	فيه مقاس أكبر؟ **feeh m'aas akbar**

No, that's not suitable.	لا، ده مش مناسب. **laa, dah mish munaasib**

I'll take the pink one.	هاخد الوردي. **haakhud il-wardee**

4 minutes

❹ jacket

4 WORDS TO REMEMBER

5 minutes

Most adjectives can be made feminine by adding **-a** (pp.64–65), but the principal colors have a special feminine form. Familiarize yourself with these words, then test yourself using the cover flap.

red (m/f)	أحمر/حمراء **aHmar/Hamra**
white (m/f)	أبيض/بيضاء **abyaD/beiDa**
blue (m/f)	أزرق/زرقاء **azra'/zar'a**
yellow (m/f)	أصفر/صفراء **asfar/Safra**
green (m/f)	أخضر/خضراء **akhDar/khaDra**
black (m/f)	أسود/سوداء **iswid/sooda**

5 SAY IT

2 minutes

I'll take the yellow one.

Do you have this in black?

Do you have a smaller size?

I want a shirt.

RaagiA wi karrar
REVIEW AND REPEAT

il-agweba *Answers*
(Cover with flap)

Bazzar

❶ جلابية
galabeyya

❷ أبريق
Abreeq

❸ قنديل
qandeel

❹ فانوس
fanoos

❺ تمثال
timsaal

---

1 BAZAAR

3 minutes

Name these items in Arabic.

❶ robe **❷** pitcher **❸** chandelier

lantern **❹** **❺** statue

Description

❶ The shirt is a little expensive.

❷ The room is very small.

❸ We want a large car.

---

2 DESCRIPTION

2 minutes

What do these sentences mean?

❶ il-amees ghalee shwayya

❷ il-ghurfa sughayyara giddan

❸ eHna Aawzeen Aarabyya kibeera

Shops

❶ مخبز
makhbaz

❷ جواهرجي
gawahirgee

❸ مكتبة
maktaba

❹ محل سمك
maHal samak

❺ حلواني
Halawaanee

❻ جزار
gazzaar

---

3 SHOPS

3 minutes

Name these shops in Arabic.

❶ bakery

❷ jeweler

❸ bookstore

❹ fishmonger

❺ pastry shop

❻ butcher

4 SUPERMARKET

3 minutes

Name these products
in Arabic.

❶ household products

❷ beauty products

❸ drinks

❹ dairy products

❺ frozen foods

Supermarket

❶ منتجات منزلية
muntagaat manzileyya

❷ منتجات تجميل
muntagaat tagmeel

❸ مشروبات
mashroobaat

❹ منتجات ألبان
muntagaat albaan

❺ منتجات مجمدة
muntagaat mugammada

5 MUSEUM

4 minutes

You are buying entrance tickets at a museum.
Join in the conversation, replying in Arabic
with the help of the numbered English prompts.

ayyi khidma?
❶ We want five entrance tickets.

alf metein we khamseen geneih, min faDlak
❷ That's very expensive!

shaamil gawla maA daleel
❸ Okay. Five tickets, please.

itfaDDal
❹ Here you go. Is there an elevator?

aywah. il-asanseir hinaak
❺ Where are the restrooms?

hinaak, Alaa el-shemaal
❻ Thank you very much.

Museum

❶ عاوزين خمس تذاكر دخول.
Aawizeen khamas tadhaakir dukhool

❷ ده غالي جدا!
dah ghaali giddan

❸ ماشي. خمس تذاكر من فضلك.
maashi. khamas tazaakir min faDlak(-ik)

❹ اتفضل. فيه أسانسير؟
itfaDDal. feeh asanseir

❺ شكرا. فين الحمامات؟
shukran. fein il-Hammaamaat

❻ شكرًا جزيلاً
shukran gazeelan

Ish-shughl
WORK

Ask "**Which platform?**" (pp.38–39).

What is the Arabic for these family members: "**sister**," "**brother**," "**son**," "**daughter**," "**mother**," and "**father**"? (pp.10–11).

Most job titles are masculine and can be turned into the feminine equivalent by adding the suffix **-a**—for example, **doktoor/doktoora** (*male/female doctor*). When a job title is a compound word, the ending of the first word changes to form the feminine—for example, **saaheb maHal/saahbat maHal** (*male/female shopkeeper*).

2 ◀)) **WORDS TO REMEMBER**: JOBS
7 minutes

Familiarize yourself with these words, then test yourself using the cover flap. The feminine form is also shown.

دكتور/دكتورة **doktoor/doktoora**	doctor (m/f)
دكتور/دكتورة أسنان **doktoor/doktoorit asnaan**	dentist (m/f)
ممرض/ممرضة **mumarriD/mumarriDa**	nurse (m/f)
مدرس/مدرسة **mudarris/mudarrisa**	teacher (m/f)
محاسب/محاسبة **muHaasib/muHaasba**	accountant (m/f)
محام/محامية **muHaami/muHaameyya**	lawyer (m/f)
مصمم/مصممة **musammim/musammima**	designer (m/f)
محرر/محررة **muHarrir/muHarrira**	editor (m/f)
رجل أعمال/سيدة أعمال **raagil aAmaal/ sayyidit aAmaal**	businessman/ businesswoman
سكرتير/سكرتيرة **sekerteir/sekerteira**	secretary (m/f)
كهربائي **kahrabaa'ee**	electrician
سباك **sabbaak**	plumber
طباخ/طباخة **Tabbaakh/Tabbaakha**	cook/chef (m/f)
مهندس/مهندسة **muhandes/muhandisa**	engineer (m/f)
عامل حر **Aamel Hor**	self-employed

أنا سباك.
ana sabbaak
I'm a plumber.

هي طالبة.
heyya Taaliba
She is a student.

3 **PUT INTO PRACTICE**

4 minutes

Complete this dialogue, then test yourself using the cover flap. Note that when you state your occupation, you don't need the equivalent of am/are/is or a/an, as in: **ana muharrir/a** (I'm an editor).

بتشتغل إيه؟
bitishtaghal eh
What do you do?
Say: I'm a businessman.

أنا رجل أعمال.
ana raagil aAmaal

عندك شركة؟
Aandak sherka
Do you have a company?
Say: Yes. I have a small company.

أيوه، عندي شركة صغيرة.
aywah, Aandee sherka sughayyara

عظيم!
Aazeem
Great!
Say: And you, what's your job?

وأنت، بتشتغل إيه؟
wenta, bitishtaghal eh

أنا دكتور.
ana doktoor
I'm a doctor.
Say: My sister is also a doctor.

أختي كمان دكتورة.
ukhtee kamaan doktoora

4 **WORDS TO REMEMBER:**
WORKPLACE

3 minutes

الفرع الرئيسي الرئيسي في القاهرة.
elfarA ir-ra'eesee fil qaahira
The head office is in Cairo.

Familiarize yourself with these words, then test yourself using the cover flap.

head office	الفرع الرئيسي **elfarA ir-ra'eesee**
branch	فرع **farA**
department	قسم **qism**
manager	مدير **mudeer**
employee	موظف **muwazzaf**
trainee	تحت التمرين **taHt it-tamreen**

Il-maktab
THE OFFICE

(pp.8–9, pp.14–15, and pp.78–79).

1 WARM UP — 1 minute

Practice different ways of introducing yourself in different situations. Say your name, occupation, and any other information you'd like to give (pp.8–9, pp.14–15, and pp.78–79).

An office environment or business situation has its own vocabulary in any language, but there are many items for which the terminology is virtually universal. Note that Arabic computer keyboards show the individual letters (pp.152–156) and the software joins the letters as you type.

2 WORDS TO REMEMBER — 5 minutes

Familiarize yourself with these words, then test yourself using the cover flap.

اجتماع **igtimaaA**	meeting
ماكينة تصوير **makanit tasweer**	copier
كمبيوتر **kompyootar**	computer
شاشة **shaasha**	monitor/screen
ماوس **mawus**	mouse
انترنت **internet**	internet
ايميل **email**	email
كلمة المرور **kilmit il-muroor**	password
كلمة مرور الواي فاي **kilmit muroor il wifi**	Wi-Fi password
مؤتمر **mu'tamar**	conference
نوتة **nota**	notebook
أجندة **ajenda**	calendar
كارت شخصي **kart shakhSee**	business card
رسالة صوتية **risaala sawteyya**	voicemail

3 MATCH

- ① wall clock
- ④ telephone
- ③ stapler
- ⑩ pen
- ⑨ notebook
- ⑪ drawer

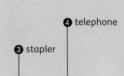

4 USEFUL PHRASES

2 minutes

Learn these phrases, then test yourself using the cover flap.

I (f) want to send an email.
عاوزة ابعث ايميل.
Aawza abAat email

---

5 SAY IT

2 minutes

I want to arrange a meeting.

Do you have a business card?

Can I use the copier?
ممكن استخدم ماكينة التصوير؟
mumkin astakhdam maakanit it-taSweer

I (m) want to make an appointment.
عاوز آخذ ميعاد.
Aawiz aakhud miAaad

AND REPEAT

5 minutes

Match the numbered items to the list, then test yourself using the cover flap.

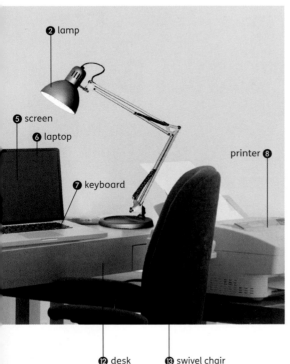

2 lamp
5 screen
6 laptop
7 keyboard
printer **8**
12 desk
13 swivel chair

1 ساعة حائط
saaAet HeiTa

2 لمبة
lamba

3 دباسة
dabbaasa

4 تليفون
tilifoon

5 شاشة
shaasha

6 لابتوب
laabtob

7 كيبورد
keeboord

8 ماكينة طباعة
makanit TebaaAa

9 نوتة
nota

10 قلم
alam

11 درج
dorg

12 مكتب
maktab

13 كرسي دوّار
kursee dawaar

Il-Aalam il-akaadeemee
ACADEMIC WORLD

In most Arabic-speaking countries, students
are selected for a first degree according
to their results in final high school exams.
Competition for places in fields such as
medicine and engineering is often fierce.

2 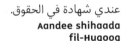 | **USEFUL PHRASES**

3 minutes

Practice these phrases, then test yourself using the cover flap.

مجالك إيه؟
magaalak/-ik eh

What is your field?
(m/f)

بعمل أبحاث في الكيميا
الحيوية
**baAmel abHaath fee
el-kimia el-Hayaweyya**

I am doing research
in biochemistry.

عندي شهادة في الحقوق.
**Aandee shihaada
fil-Huqooq**

I have a bachelor's
degree in law.

حالقي محاضرة عن المعمار.
**halqee muHaDra
Aan il-miAmaar**

I'm going to give a
lecture on architecture.

3 | **IN CONVERSATION**

أهلا، أنا أستاذة
هالة شوقي.
**ahlan, ana ustaaza
haala shawqi**

Hello, I'm Professor
Hala Shawqi.

من أي جامعة؟
min ayyi gamAa

From which university?

من جامعة اسكندرية.
**min gamAit
iskendereyya**

From the University
of Alexandria.

4 WORDS TO REMEMBER

4 minutes

Familiarize yourself with these words, then test yourself using the cover flap.

conference	مؤتمر	**mu'tamar**
trade fair	معرض تجاري	**maAraD tugaaree**
seminar	حلقة دراسية	**Halaqa diraasyya**
lecture	محاضرة	**muHaDra**
lecture hall	قاعة محاضرات	**qaaAit muHaDraat**
exhibition	معرض	**maAraD**
university lecturer	مُحاضر جامعي	**muHaaDer gaamAee**
professor	أستاذ	**ustaaz**
medicine	طب	**Tibb**
science	علوم	**Auloom**
arts	آداب	**aadaab**
literature	أدب	**adab**
engineering	هندسة	**handasa**

عندنا جناح في المعرض التجاري.
Aandina ginaaH fil-maAraD it-tugaaree
We have a stand at the trade fair.

5 SAY IT

2 minutes

I do research in medicine.

I have a degree in engineering.

Where's the lecture hall?

---

5 minutes

مجالك إيه؟
magaalik eh
What's your field?

أبحاث في هندسة البترول.
abHaath fi handasit il-betrool
Research in petro-engineering.

عظيم! وأنا كمان.
Aazeem. wana kamaan
Great! Me too.

1 | WARM UP
1 minute

Say **"I'm a trainee"**
(pp.78–79).

Say **"I want to send
an email"** (pp.80–81).

Say **"I want to arrange
an appointment"**
(pp.80–81).

Fil-aAmaal
IN BUSINESS

While on business trips to the MENA region,
you will make a good impression and receive a
more friendly reception if you make the effort
to begin meetings with a short introduction
in Arabic, even if your vocabulary is limited.
After that, everyone will probably be happy
to continue the meeting in English.

2 WORDS TO REMEMBER

Familiarize yourself with these words, then test yourself using the cover flap.

جدول **gadwal**	schedule
تسليم **tasleem**	delivery
دفع **dafA**	payment
ميزانية **mizaaneyya**	budget
سعر **siAr**	price
مستند **mustanad**	document
فاتورة **fatoora**	invoice
المبلغ التقديري **elmablagh el-taqdeeree**	estimate
عرض **AarD**	proposal
أرباح **arbaaH**	profits
مبيعات **mabeeAaat**	sales
أرقام **arqaam**	figures

مدير
mudeer
manager —

عقد
Aa'd
contract

نمضي العقد؟
nimDee il-Aa'd
Shall we sign the
contract?

3 🔊 USEFUL PHRASES

6 minutes

Learn these phrases, then test yourself using the cover flap.

ابعث لي العقد من فضلك.
ibAatlee il-Aa'd min faDlak

Please send me the contract.

اتفقنا على الجدول؟
ittafa'na Aalal gadwal

Have we agreed to a schedule?

ميعاد التسليم امتى؟
miAaad it-tasleem imta

When is the delivery date?

الميزانية كام؟
il-mizaaneyya kaam

How much is the budget?

ممكن تبعتلي الفاتورة؟
mumkin tebAatlee el fatoora

Can you send me the invoice? (to a man)

6 minutes

عميل
Aameel
client

تقرير
taqreer
report

4 SAY IT

2 minutes

Please send me the schedule.

Have we agreed to a price?

How much is the invoice?

RaagiA wi karrar
REVIEW AND REPEAT

At the office

❶ ساعة حيطة
saaAet Heita

❷ لابتوب
laabtob

❸ لمبة
lamba

❹ ماكينة طباعة
makanit TebaaAa

❺ دباسة
dabbaasa

❻ قلم
alam

❼ نوتة
nota

❽ مكتب
maktab

Jobs

❶ دكتور
doktoor

❷ سباك
sabbaak

❸ طباخ
Tabbaakh

❹ محاسب
muHaasib

❺ طالب
Taalib

❻ محام
muHaami

1 AT THE OFFICE

Name these items in Arabic.

wall clock ❶   ❷ laptop   ❸ lamp

❺ stapler   pen ❻   ❼ notebook   ❽ desk

2 JOBS

3 minutes

Name these jobs in Arabic.

❶ doctor
❷ plumber
❸ cook/chef
❹ accountant
❺ student
❻ lawyer

4 minutes

4 printer

3 WORK

4 minutes

Answer these questions following
the numbered English prompts.

bitishtaghal eh?
❶ I am a university lecturer.

min ayyi gamAa?
❷ From Cairo University.

magaalak eh?
❸ Research in medicine.

Halqee muHaDra innahaarda
❹ Great! Me too.

Work
❶ أنا أستاذ جامعي.
ana ustaaz gaamAee
❷ من جامعة القاهرة.
min gamAit al-qaahira
❸ أبحاث في الطب.
abHaath fiT-Tibb
❹ عظيم! وأنا كمان.
Aazeem. wana kamaan

4 HOW MUCH?

4 minutes

Answer these questions in Arabic using
the amounts given in brackets.

❶ **bikaam il-ahwa?** (50 pounds)
❷ **bikaam il-ghurfa?** (6000 pounds)
❸ **bikaam il-galabeyya?** (200 pounds)
❹ **bikaam ir-riHla?** (2500 pounds)

How much?
❶ خمسين جنيه
khamseen gineih
❷ ستلاف جنيه
sittalaaf gineih
❸ ميتين جنيه
meLein gineih
❹ ألفين وخمسميت جنيه
alfein we khomsomeet gineih

1 WARM UP
1 minute

Say "I'm allergic to nuts" (pp.22–23).

Say "I have," "he has," "she has," and "do you have?" (masculine/feminine) (pp.14–15).

Il-gism
THE BODY

You are most likely to need to refer to parts of the body in the context of illness—for example, when describing a problem to a doctor. A useful phrase for talking about aches and pain is **Aandee alam fi...** (*I have a pain in...*). To ask someone *what's the matter?*, say **maalak?** when talking to a man and **maalik?** to a woman.

2 MATCH AND REPEAT: BODY
6 minutes

Match the numbered parts of the body to the list, then test yourself using the cover flap.

❶ رأس
raas

❷ شعر
shaAr

❸ كتف
kitf

❹ رقبة
ra'aba

❺ ذراع
diraaA

❻ صدر
sidr

❼ يد
yad

❽ كوع
kooA

❾ بطن
baTn

❿ رجل
rigl

⓫ ركبة
rukba

⓬ قدم
qadam

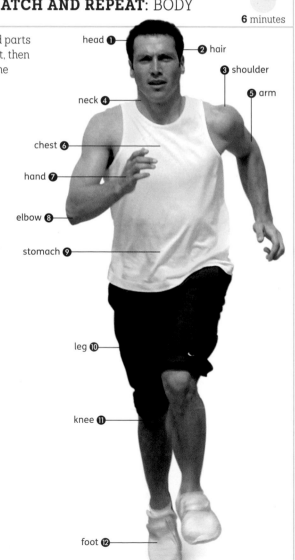

head ❶
❷ hair
❸ shoulder
❺ arm
neck ❹
chest ❻
hand ❼
elbow ❽
stomach ❾
leg ❿
knee ⓫
foot ⓬

3 MATCH AND REPEAT: FACE

3 minutes

Match the numbered facial features to the list, then test yourself using the cover flap.

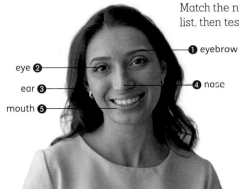

- ❶ eyebrow
- eye ❷
- ear ❸
- ❹ nose
- mouth ❺

❶ حاجب
Haagib

❷ عين
Aein

❸ أذن
uzun

❹ أنف
anf

❺ فم
fam

4 USEFUL PHRASES

3 minutes

Learn these phrases, then test yourself using the cover flap.

I have a pain in my back. — عندي ألم في ظهري.
Aandee alam fi Dahree

I have a swollen area on my arm. — عندي ورم في ذراعي.
Aandee waram fi diraaAee

I don't feel well. — عندي شعور بالتعب.
Aandee shuAoor bit-taAb

5 PUT INTO PRACTICE

2 minutes

Complete this dialogue, then test yourself using the cover flap.

مالك؟ عندي شعور بالتعب.
maalik Aandee shuAoor bit-taAb

What's the matter?
Say: I don't feel well.

فين الألم؟ عندي ألم في كتفي.
fein il-alam Aandee alam fi kitfee

Where does it hurt?
Say: I have a pain in my shoulder.

Fis-Saydaleyya
AT THE PHARMACY

<table>
<tr><td>

1 **WARM UP**

1 minute

Say "**I have a swollen area on my arm**" and "**I don't feel well**" (pp.88–89).

Say the Arabic for "**red**," "**green**," "**black**," and "**yellow**" (masculine/feminine) (pp.74–75).

</td></tr>
</table>

Pharmacies are often indicated by a serpent-entwined rod. Pharmacists are qualified to give advice about minor health problems and are permitted to dispense both prescription and over-the-counter medicines (**dawa** in Arabic). You may also be able to buy strong painkillers and antibiotics from a pharmacy, but it is always advisable to consult a doctor first.

2 MATCH AND REPEAT

3 minutes

Match the numbered items to the list, then test yourself using the cover flap.

❶ رباط
robaaT

❷ دوا شُرب
dawa shorb

❸ نقط
nu'aT

❹ كريم
kreem

❺ بلاستر
blaaster

❻ حقنة
Hu'na

❼ لبوس
loboos

❽ حبوب
Huboob

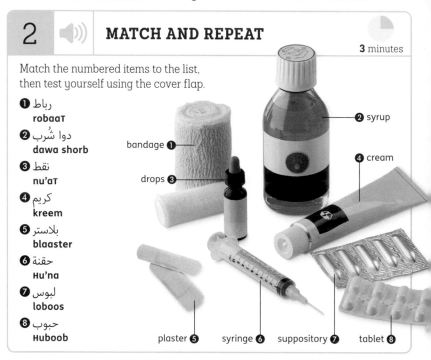

bandage ❶
drops ❸
❷ syrup
❹ cream
plaster ❺   syringe ❻   suppository ❼   tablet ❽

3 IN CONVERSATION

صباح الخير.
أي خدمة؟
sabaaH il-kheir. ayyi khidma

Good morning. Can I help you?

عندي مغص.
Aandee maghas

I have a stomach ache.

عندك إسهال؟
Aandak ishaal

Do you have diarrhea?

4 WORDS TO REMEMBER

2 minutes

Familiarize yourself with these words, then test yourself using the flap.

عندي صداع.
Aandee SodaaA
I have a headache.

headache	صداع **SodaaA**
stomach ache	مغص **maghas**
diarrhea	إسهال **ishaal**
cold	برد **bard**
cough	كحة **koHHa**
sunstroke	ضربة شمس **Darbit shams**
toothache	ألم أسنان **alam asnaan**

5 USEFUL PHRASES

4 minutes

Learn these phrases, then test yourself using the cover flap.

Do you have face masks?	فيه كمامات؟ **feeh kimamaat**
Do you have that as drops?	عندكم ده نقط؟ **Aandakum dah nu'at**
I'm allergic to penicillin.	عندي حساسية للبنسلين. **Aandee Hassaaseyya lil-binsileen**

6 SAY IT

2 minutes

I have a cold.

Do you have that as a cream?

He has a toothache.

---

3 minutes

لا، بس عندي صداع.
laa, bass Aandee SodaaA

No, but I have a headache.

جرب ده.
garrab dah

Try this.

عندكم ده حبوب؟
Aandukum dah Huboob

Do you have that as tablets?

Aand id-doktoor
AT THE DOCTOR

1 WARM UP

1 minute

Say "**I need some tablets**" and "**We need some cream**" (pp.60–61 and pp.64–65).

What is the Arabic for "**I don't have a son**"? (pp.14–15).

In an emergency, call for an ambulance (look up the local number before you travel, or ask your hotel for help). If it isn't urgent, book an appointment with the doctor. You can pay at the clinic either while booking the appointment or just before seeing the doctor. You can usually get the money back if you have comprehensive travel and medical insurance.

2 USEFUL PHRASES YOU MAY HEAR

3 minutes

Learn these phrases, then test yourself using the cover flap.

الحالة مش خطيرة.
il-Haala mish khaTeera
It's not serious.

هاكتب لك/لك روشتة.
hakteb lak/lik roshetta
I'm going to write you (m/f) a prescription.

عندك التهاب.
Aandak/-ik iltihaab
You have (m/f) an infection.

لازم تروح/تروحي المستشفى.
laazim tirooH/tirooHee il-mustashfa
You must go to the hospital.

افتح بؤك من فضلك.
iftaH bo'ak min faDlak
Open your mouth, please. (to a man)

افتحي بؤك من فضلك.
iftaHee bo'ik min faDlik
Open your mouth, please. (to a woman)

لازم نعمل شوية تحاليل.
laazim neAmel shwayyit taHaaleel
We have to do some tests.

3 IN CONVERSATION

بتشتكي من إيه؟
bitishkee min eh
What's the problem?

عندي ألم في صدري.
Aandee alam fi sidree
I have a pain in my chest.

اكشف عليكي من فضلك.
akshif Aaleikee min faDlik
Let me examine you, please.

4 USEFUL PHRASES YOU MAY NEED TO SAY

4 minutes

Learn these phrases, then test yourself using the cover flap.

أنا حامل.
ana Haamil
I'm pregnant.

I have diabetes.	عندي السكر. **Aandee is-sukkar**
I have epilepsy.	عندي صرع. **Aandee Sa-raA**
I have asthma.	عندي ربو. **Aandee rabwu**
I have a heart condition.	عندي مشكلة في القلب. **Aandee mushkila fil-alb**
I'm feeling (m/f) faint.	حاسس/حاسة بالضعف. **Hasis/Haassa biDaAf**
I have a fever.	عندي حرارة. **Aandee Haraara**
It's urgent.	الحالة مستعجلة. **il-Haala mistaAgila**
I'm here for my vaccination.	عاوز/عاوزة آخد اللقاح. **Aawiz/Aawza aakhud il-liqaaH**

Cultural tip Most doctors are likely to speak English, but support staff may not. When calling for an appointment, be prepared in case you need to briefly explain your problem in Arabic to a receptionist or nurse. Be mindful of cultural differences. Some doctors in more conservative areas and smaller towns may avoid eye contact with patients of the opposite gender as this is seen as culturally respectful.

5 SAY IT

2 minutes

My son has diabetes.

I have a pain in my arm.

It's not urgent.

Do I need tests?

---

5 minutes

الحالة خطيرة؟
il-Haala khaTeera
Is it serious?

لا، عندك عسر هضم بس.
laa, Aandik Ausr haDm bass
No, you only have indigestion.

طمنتني!
Tammintinee
What a relief!

1 **WARM UP**

1 minute

Ask "**How far is it?**" (pp.42–43).

Say "**I have to do some tests**" (pp.38–39).

What is the Arabic for "**mouth**" and "**head**"? (pp.88–89).

Fil-mustashfa
AT THE HOSPITAL

When visiting the MENA region, you should make sure to have comprehensive travel and medical insurance to cover any treatment or hospital stay, although in some places these are affordable even when paid out of pocket. It is useful to know a few basic phrases relating to hospitals for use in an emergency, or if you need to visit a friend or colleague in the hospital.

2 🔊 **USEFUL PHRASES**

5 minutes

Learn these phrases, then test yourself using the cover flap.

إيه مواعيد الزيارة؟
eh mawaaAeed iz-ziyaara
What are the visiting hours?

هل الحلقة السمعية متوفرة؟
Hal il Halaqa AssamAia motawaffira?
Is a hearing loop available?

حتأخذ وقت قد إيه؟
hatakhud wa't ad eh
How long will it take?

هتألم؟
Hat-allim
Will it hurt?

نام هنا من فضلك.
naam hina, min faDlak
Lie down here, please. (to a man)

نامي هنا من فضلك.
naamee hina, min faDlik
Lie down here, please. (to a woman)

ما تاكلش/ تاكليش حاجة.
maa takulsh/ takleesh Haaga
Don't eat anything. (to a man/woman)

متحركش راسك.
matHarraksh raasak
Don't move your head. (to a man)

متحركيش راسِك.
matHarrakeesh raasik
Don't move your head. (to a woman)

لازم نعمل تحليل دم.
laazim neAmel taHleel dam
We have to do a blood test.

فين غرفة الانتظار؟
fein ghurfit il-intiZaar
Where is the waiting room?

أنت أحسن؟
enti aHsan
Are you feeling better?

3 WORDS TO REMEMBER

4 minutes

Familiarize yourself with these words, then test yourself using the cover flap.

صورة الأشعة طبيعية.
soorit il-ashiAa TabeeAeyya
Your x-ray is normal.

emergency room	قسم الطوارئ **qism iT-Tawaari'**
x-ray department	قسم الأشعة **qism il-ashiAa**
children's ward	عنبر الأطفال **Aanbar il-aTfaal**
operating room	غرفة العمليات **ghurfit il-Aamaliyyaat**
waiting room	غرفة الانتظار **ghurfit il-intizaar**
elevator	أسانسير **asanseir**
stairs	سلم **sillim**

4 PUT INTO PRACTICE

3 minutes

Complete this dialogue, then test yourself using the cover flap.

عندك التهاب في الكلى. **Aandak iltihaab fil-kila** الحالة خطيرة؟ **il-Haala khaTeera**
You have a kidney infection.
Ask: Is it serious?

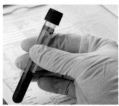

لازم نعمل تحليل دم. **laazim neAmel taHleel dam** هتألم؟ **Hat-allim**
We have to do a blood test.
Ask: Will it hurt?

5 SAY IT

2 minutes

We have to do a blood test.

Where is the children's ward?

Do I need an x-ray?

لا متقلقش. **laa maate'la'sh** هياخد وقت أد إيه؟ **hayakhud wa't 'ad eh?**
No, don't worry.
Ask: How long will it take?

RaagiA wi karrar
REVIEW AND REPEAT

The body

❶ رأس
raas

❷ ذراع
diraaA

❸ صدر
sidr

❹ بطن
baTn

❺ رجل
rigl

❻ ركبة
rukba

❼ قدم
qadam

On the phone

❶ ممكن أكلم الأستاذ سالم؟
**mumkin akallim
il-ustaaz
saalim**

❷ عدنان علي من
مطابع .كابيتال
**Adnan Ali min
maTaabiA kabitaal**

❸ ممكن أسيب رسالة؟
mumkin aseeb risaala

❹ الاجتماع الساعة تسعة.
**il-igtimaaA
issaaAa tisAa**

❺ مع السلامة.
maAasalaama

1 THE BODY
4 minutes

Name these body parts in Arabic.

❶ head
❷ arm
chest ❸
stomach ❹
leg ❺
knee ❻
❼ foot

2 ON THE PHONE
4 minutes

You are arranging an appointment. Join in the conversation, replying in Arabic following the numbered English prompts.

**aaloh. maAak
Azza barakaat**
❶ Can I speak to
Mr. Saalim?

meen maAaya?
❷ Adnan Ali from
Capital Printers.

il-khaT mashghool
❸ Can I leave a message?

tabAan
❹ The meeting is
at 9 o'clock.

tamaam. shukran
❺ Goodbye.

il-agweba *Answers*
(Cover with flap)

3 CLOTHING

3 minutes

Name these items of clothing in Arabic.

tie ❶

❷ jacket

pocket ❸

❹ pants

shoes ❺

Clothing

❶ كرافتة
kravatta

❷ جاكتة
jaketta

❸ جيب
geib

❹ بنطلون
banTaloon

❺ جزمة
gazma

4 AT THE DOCTOR'S

4 minutes

Say these sentences
in Arabic.

❶ I don't feel well.

❷ I have diabetes.

❸ I have a pain in
my shoulder.

❹ I'm pregnant.

❺ I'm here for
my vaccination.

At the doctor's

❶ عندي شعور بالتعب.
**Aandee shuAoor
bit-taAb**

❷ عندي السكر.
Aandee is-sukkar

❸ عندي ألم في كتفي.
**Aandee alam fi
kitfee**

❹ أنا حامل.
ana Haamil

❺ عاوز/عاوزة آخد.
اللقاح.
**Aawiz/Aawza
aakhud il-liqaaH**

1 WARM UP

1 minute

Say the months of the year in Arabic (pp.28–29).

Ask "**Is there an art gallery?**" (pp.48–49) and "**How many brothers do you have?**" (pp.14–15).

Fil-beit
AT HOME

Many city dwellers live in apartments (**shu'a'**) in low-rise blocks (**Aomaraat**), towers (**abraag**), and skyscrapers (**naaTiHaat saHaab**), while suburbs, tourist resorts, and rural areas often have traditional detached houses (**biyout**) and villas (**villaat**) with gardens. A neighborhood is called **Hay**, the city center is **weST il-balad**, and a suburb is **manTe'a**.

2 MATCH AND REPEAT

Match the numbered items to the list, then test yourself using the cover flap.

❶ سطح
satH

❷ شباك
shibbaak

❸ برجولة
bergoola

❹ بلكونة
balkoona

❺ سلالم
salaalim

❻ باب
baab

❼ حائط
HeiTa

❽ مدخل
madkhal

❶ roof   ❷ window   ❸ pergola

stairs ❺   door ❻

Cultural tip Most homes in the Arabic-speaking world have shutters (**sheesh**) on every window and balcony door. These are closed at night and in the heat of the day. You might see antique shutters in some areas, but you are likely to see modern ones in most urban areas. Curtains, where they are present, tend to be more for decoration. Many windows also have mesh screens to protect against mosquitoes and other insects.

الإيجار كام في الشهر؟
il-eegaar kaam fish-shahr
What is the monthly rent?

5 minutes

 4 balcony

7 wall   **8** driveway

3 USEFUL PHRASES

3 minutes

Learn these phrases, then test yourself using the cover flap.

فيها تكييف؟
feehaa takyeef

Is there air-conditioning?

فاضية دلوقتي؟
faDya dilwa'ti

Is it vacant now?

الفيلا مفروشة؟
il-villa mafroosha

Is the villa furnished?

4 WORDS TO REMEMBER

4 minutes

Familiarize yourself with these words, then test yourself using the cover flap.

room	غرفة **ghurfa**
floor	أرضية **arDeyya**
ceiling	سقف **sa'f**
bedroom	غرفة نوم **ghurfit noom**
bathroom	حمام **Hammaam**
living room	غرفة جلوس **ghurfit guloos**
dining room	غرفة سفرة **ghurfit sufra**
kitchen	مطبخ **maTbakh**
garage	جراج **garaaj**

5 SAY IT

2 minutes

Is there a dining room?

Is the apartment furnished?

Is it vacant in July?

1 WARM UP
1 minute

What is the Arabic for "**table**" (pp.20–21), "**room**" (pp.58–59), "**desk**" (pp.80–81), "**bed**" (pp.60–61), and "**window**"? (pp.98–99).

How do you say "**beautiful**," "**old**," and "**big**"? (pp.64–65).

Villas or apartments can be rented furnished or unfurnished. You will need to check in advance with the **simsaar** (*agent*) or homeowner to see if the cost of utilities such as electricity and water is included in the rent. You may also need to pay a share of the fee for the upkeep of the communal areas and sometimes contribute to the cost of employing a **bawwaab** (*doorman*).

2 MATCH AND REPEAT
3 minutes

Match the numbered items to the list, then test yourself using the cover flap.

❶ ثلاجة
tallaaga

❷ بوتاجاز
butagaaz

❸ حوض
HooD

❹ سطح المطبخ
saTh il-maTbakh

❺ ميكرويف
mikroweiv

❻ فرن
furn

❼ سفرة
sufra

❽ كرسي
kursee

fridge ❶ stove ❷ sink ❸ ❹ counter

microwave ❺ oven ❻ table ❼ ❽ chair

3 IN CONVERSATION

ده الفرن.
dah el-furn
This is the oven.

فيه غسالة أطباق كمان؟
feh ghassalit aTbaa' kaman
Is there a dishwasher as well?

أيوه، وهنا فريزر كبير.
aywah, wi-hina freezar kibeer
Yes, and there's a big freezer.

4 WORDS TO REMEMBER

2 minutes

Familiarize yourself with these words, then test yourself using the cover flap.

wardrobe	دولاب **doolaab**
armchair	كرسي بمساند للذراعين **kursee bemasaaned lil-deraaAeen**
chest of drawers	مجموعة ادراج **magmooAet adraag**
rug	سجادة **siggaada**
bathtub	بانيو **banyo**
toilet	تواليت **twaalett**
wash basin	حوض حمام **HOOD Hammaam**
curtains	ستاير **sataayir**

الكنبة جديدة.
il-kanaba gideeda
The sofa is new.

5 USEFUL PHRASES

4 minutes

Learn these phrases, then test yourself using the cover flap.

Is electricity included?	ده شامل الكهرباء؟ **dah shaamil ik-kahrabaa**
The rug isn't clean.	السجادة مش نظيفة. **is-siggaada mish niDeefa**
The stove isn't working.	البوتاجاز مش شغال. **il-butagaaz mish shagh-ghaal**

6 SAY IT

2 minutes

Is there a microwave?
The sofa isn't clean.
The oven isn't working.

3 minutes

الحوض ده جديد؟
el HOOD dah gedeed
Is the sink new?

أيوة. ودي الغسالة.
aywah wede el-ghassala
Yes. And here's the washing machine.

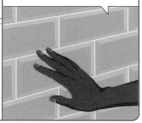

السيراميك جميل أوي
issirameek gameel awee
What beautiful tiles!

Il-gineina
THE GARDEN

1 **WARM UP**
1 minute

Say "**I need**" and "**we need**" (pp.60–61 and pp.64–65).

What is the Arabic for "**day**," "**week**," and "**month**"? (pp.28–29).

Ask "**Is the wardrobe included?**" (pp.100–101).

The garden of a block of apartments may be communal or partly shared, while houses generally have private gardens. A small fee for the upkeep of the garden may sometimes be included in the rent of an apartment. Check in advance with the agent or homeowner. In the Middle East, gardens are usually watered in the late afternoon or evening, after the hottest part of the day has passed.

---

2 **WORDS TO REMEMBER**
3 minutes

Familiarize yourself with these words, then test yourself using the cover flap.

ماكينة قص الحشيش
makanit ass il-Hasheesh
lawn mower

شوكة
shooka
rake

جاروف
gaaroof
spade

رشاش
rash-shaash
sprinkler

---

3 **MATCH AND REPEAT**

Match the numbered items to the list, then test yourself using the cover flap.

tree ❶
path ❷
plants ❸
rocks ❹
pond ❺

4 USEFUL PHRASES

4 minutes

Learn these phrases, then test yourself using the cover flap.

Is the garden private?	الجنينة خاصة؟ **il-gineina khaassa**
The gardener comes on Sunday.	الجنايني بييجي يوم الحد. **il-ganaaynee biyeegee yoom il-Had**
Can you mow the lawn?	ممكن تقص الحشيش؟ **mumkin ti'uss il-Hasheesh**
We need to water the garden.	عاوزين نسقي الجنينة. **Aawzeen nis'ee il-gineina**

5 SAY IT

2 minutes

We need to water the plants.

The palm is beautiful!

The gardener comes on Thursday.

---

5 minutes

6 palm

7 umbrella

8 flowers

9 bridge

10 hedge

1	شجرة	shagara
2	ممر	mamarr
3	زرع	zarA
4	صخور	sokhoor
5	بركة	birka
6	نخلة	nakhla
7	شمسية	shamseyya
8	ورد	ward
9	كوبري	kubree
10	سور شجري	soor shagaree

Il-Haywaanaat
ANIMALS

Say "**My name is John**" (pp.8–9).

How do you say "**Don't worry**"? (pp.94–95).

What is "**fish**" in Arabic? (pp.22–23).

Traditionally, Arabs have valued horses for their speed, camels for their stamina, and birds of prey for their grace. Nowadays, smaller dogs, birds, and fish are popular as house pets in the MENA region. You may also encounter stray dogs and feral cats roaming the streets—give them a wide berth and they will generally avoid you.

2 **MATCH AND REPEAT**

Match the numbered animals to the list, then test yourself using the cover flap.

❶ قطة
oTTa

❷ سمكة
samaka

❸ حصان
HuSaan

❹ عصفور
Aasfoor

❺ كلب
kalb

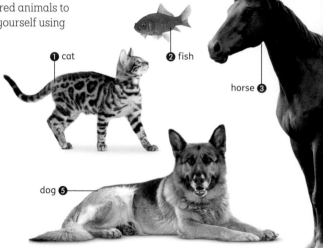

❶ cat   ❷ fish

horse ❸

dog ❺

3 **USEFUL PHRASES**

4 minutes

Learn these phrases, then test yourself using the cover flap.

الكلب ده أليف؟
il-kalb dah aleef — Is this dog friendly?

ممكن أجيب كلب الإرشاد بتاعي معايا؟
momken ageeb kalb il-ershaad betaaAee maAaaya — Can I bring my guide dog?

أنا مش غاوي/غاوية قطط.
ana mish ghaawee/ ghaawya oTaT — I'm not fond (m/f) of cats.

الكلب ده ما بيعضش.
il-kalb dah mabyAoDDish — This dog doesn't bite.

الجمل ده بيعض؟
il-gamal dah byAoDD
Does this camel bite?

Cultural tip Large dogs are sometimes kept outside as working or guard dogs rather than treated as indoor pets. Keep away from the dog's territory, and approach with care if necessary. Look out for warning notices such as **iнtaris min elkelaab** (*beware of the dog*). Never refer to anyone as a dog, donkey, or any animal—this is considered very insulting.

احترس من الكلاب

3 minutes

bird **4**

4 ◀)) WORDS TO REMEMBER

4 minutes

Familiarize yourself with these words, then test yourself using the cover flap.

water buffalo	جاموسة **gamoosa**	
sheep	خروف **kharoof**	
cow	بقرة **ba'ara**	
donkey	حمار **Humaar**	
rabbit	أرنب **arnab**	
vet	دكتور بيطري **doktoor beTaree**	
bowl	طبق أكل للكلب **Taba' akl lil-kalb**	
collar	طوق الكلب **Too' il-kalb**	
leash	حبل **Habl**	

السمكة دي نوعها أيه؟
is-samaka dee nowAha eh
What type of fish is that?

5 ◀)) PUT INTO PRACTICE

3 minutes

Complete this dialogue, then test yourself using the cover flap.

ده كلبك؟ اسمه إيه؟
dah kalbik? ismuh eh

أيوه، اسمه لاكي.
aywah, ismuh laakee

Is this your dog?
What's his name?

Say: Yes. His name is Lucky.

أنا مش غاوي كلاب.
ana mish ghaawee kilaab

ما بيعضش.
mabyAoDDish

I'm not fond of dogs.

Say: He doesn't bite.

il-agweba *Answers*
(Cover with flap)

RaagiA wi karrar
REVIEW AND REPEAT

1 COLORS

4 minutes

Fill in the blanks with the correct Arabic masculine or feminine form of the color given in parentheses.

❶ **il-amees** _____ . (white)

❷ **il-banTaloon** _____ . (blue)

❸ **il-kravatta** _____ . (red)

❹ **il-ward** _____ . (yellow)

❺ **il-gazma** _____ . (black)

Colors

❶ أبيض
abyaD

❷ أزرق
azra'

❸ حمراء
Hamra

❹ أصفر
asfar

❺ سوداء
sooda

2 KITCHEN

Name these items in Arabic.

fridge ❶ stove ❷ ❸ oven ❹ sink

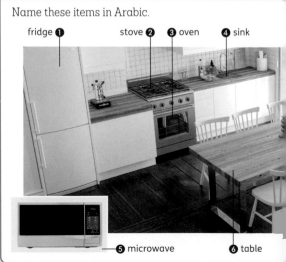

❺ microwave ❻ table

Kitchen

❶ ثلاجة
tallaaga

❷ بوتاجاز
butagaaz

❸ فرن
furn

❹ حوض
HooD

❺ ميكرويف
mikroweiv

❻ سفرة
sufra

❼ كرسي
kursee

il-agweba *Answers*
(Cover with flap)

3 HOUSE

4 minutes

You are visiting a house. Join in the conversation, asking questions in Arabic following the numbered English prompts.

ghurfit il-guloos hina
❶ The rug is beautiful!

aywah, wi-adeema giddan
❷ Is there a dining room as well?

laa, bass feeh sufra kibeera fil-maтbakh
❸ Is there a garage?

aywah, wi feeh gineina kamaan
❹ Is it vacant now?

aywah, faдya
❺ What is the monthly rent?

House
❶ السجادة جميلة!
is-siggaada gameela
❷ فيه غرفة سفرة كمان؟
feeh ghurfit sufra kamaan
❸ فيه جراج؟
feeh garaaj
❹ فاضية دلوقتي؟
faдya dilwa'ti
❺ الإيجار كام في الشهر؟
il-eegaar kaam fish-shahr

---

4 minutes

4 AT HOME

3 minutes

Name these things in Arabic.

❶ washing machine ❹ kitchen
❷ sofa ❺ tree
❸ pond ❻ garden

❼ chair

At home
❶ غسالة
ghassaala
❷ كنبة
kanaba
❸ بركة
birka
❹ مطبخ
maтbakh
❺ شجرة
shagara
❻ جنينة
gineina

Maktab Seraafa, bank, wi maktab il-bareed
CURRENCY EXCHANGE, BANK, AND MAIL

1 **WARM UP**
1 minute

Ask "**How do I get to the station?**" and "**Where is the post office?**" (pp.50–51, pp.68–69).

What's the Arabic for "**passport**"? (pp.54–55).

Ask "**What time is the meeting?**" (pp.30–31).

You can exchange currencies at a currency exchange for a better rate than your hotel's foreign exchange desk. You can also get cash at a bank ATM but may be charged a fee. The postal service in the Arabic-speaking world is variable and may be slow.

---

2 **WORDS TO REMEMBER**: MAIL

3 minutes

Familiarize yourself with these words, then test yourself using the cover flap.

صندوق بريد **Sundoo' bareed**	mail box
طوابع **TawaabiA**	stamps
طرد **Tard**	parcel
جواب **gawaab**	letter
بريد جوي **bareed gawwee**	air mail
بريد مسجل **bareed mosaggal**	registered mail
ساعي البريد **saaAee il-bareed**	mailman

بطاقة بريدية
bitaa'a bareedyya
postcard

ظرف
Zarf
envelope

بكام التكلفة للملكة المتحدة؟
bekaam ettaklifa lil-mamlaka el-mottaHeda
How much is it for the United Kingdom?

---

3  **IN CONVERSATION**: CURRENCY EXCHANGE

عاوز أغير فلوس.
Aawiz aghayyar fuloos

I would like to exchange some money.

عاوز تغير إيه؟
Aawiz teghayyar eh

What would you like to exchange?

عاوز أغير خمسمية دولار بجنيه مصري.
Aawiz aghayyar khomsomeet dolaar begeneih maSree

I would like to buy pounds for five hundred dollars.

4 WORDS TO REMEMBER: BANK

2 minutes

Familiarize yourself with these words, then test yourself using the cover flap.

bank	بنك	**bank**
ATM	ماكينة ATM	**makanit eh tee im**
PIN	الرقم السري	**erraqam esseree**
cash/money	فلوس	**fuloos**
bill	بنكنوت	**banknote**
change	فكة	**fakka**
credit card	كارت الائتمان	**kart il-i'timaan**
contactless payment	بكارت واي فاي	**becart waiy faiy**

كارت فيزا
kart viza
debit card

أدفع إزاي؟
adfaA ezzay?
How can I pay?

5 USEFUL PHRASES

4 minutes

Learn these phrases, then test yourself using the cover flap.

I'd like to exchange some money.	عاوز أصرف فلوس.	**Aawiz aSrif fuloos**
What is the exchange rate?	سعر الصرف إيه؟	**siAr is-sarf eh**
What would you like to exchange?	عاوز تغير إيه؟	**Aawiz teghayyar eh**

6 SAY IT

2 minutes

I'd like a stamp for the United Kingdom, please.

Can I pay by credit card?

Do I need my PIN?

3 minutes

تحت أمرك. معاك إثبات شخصية؟
taHt amrak. maAaak esbat shaKsyya?

Of course. Do you have any identification?

أيوه، معايا جواز السفر.
aywah, maAaya gawaaz is-safar

Yes, I have my passport.

شكرًا. اتفضل المبلغ.
shukran, itfaDDal elmablagh.

Thank you, here are your pounds.

Il-khadamaat
SERVICES

<table>
<tr><td>

1 | WARM UP

1 minute

What is the Arabic for
"It doesn't work"?
(pp.60–61).

Say **today** and
"tomorrow" in Arabic
(pp.28–29).

</td><td>

You can combine the Arabic words on these pages
with the vocabulary you learned in week 10 to
help you explain basic problems and cope with
arranging most repairs. When organizing building
work or a repair, it's a good idea to agree to a
price and method of payment in advance.

</td></tr>
</table>

2 **WORDS TO REMEMBER**

4 minutes

In the MENA region, many jobs are done only by men. The feminine form is
shown for those jobs that are also done by women. Familiarize yourself with
these words, then test yourself using the cover flap.

سباك **sabbaak**	plumber
كهربائي **kahrabaa'ee**	electrician
ميكانيكي/ميكانيكية **mikaneekee/ mikaneekyya**	mechanic (m/f)
بناء **bannaa**	builder
نقاش **na'aash**	decorator
نجار **naggaar**	carpenter
بنّا **banna**	bricklayer
عامل/عاملة نظافة **Aaamil/Aaamilit naDafa**	cleaning staff (m/f)

أنا محتاج ميكانيكي.
ana mihtaag mikaneekee
I need a mechanic.

3 **IN CONVERSATION**

غسالة الأطباق مش شغالة. **ghassaalit il-aTbaa' mish shagh-ghaala**	أيوه، الخرطوم بايظ. **aywah il-kharToom baayiz**	ممكن تصلحه؟ **mumkin tiSallaHoo**
The dishwasher doesn't work.	Yes, the hose is broken.	Can you repair it?

4 USEFUL PHRASES

3 minutes

Learn these phrases, then test yourself using the cover flap.

Can you clean the bathroom?	ممكن تنظف الحمام؟ **mumkin tinaDDaf il-Hammaam**
Can you repair the boiler?	ممكن تصلح السخان؟ **mumkin tisallaH is-sakh-khaan**
Can you repair the iron?	ممكن تصلح المكوى؟ **mumkin tisallaH il-makwa**
I'll start work tomorrow.	حابتدي شغل بكرة. **Habtidi shughl bokra**

تعرف كهربائي كويس؟
teAraf kahrabaa'ee kwayyis
Do you know a good electrician?

5 PUT INTO PRACTICE

4 minutes

Complete this dialogue, then test yourself using the cover flap.

الكرسي بايظ.
il-kursee baayiz

The chair is broken.

Ask: Can you repair it?

ممكن تصلحه؟
mumkin tisallaHoo

لا، محتاج نجار.
laa. miHtaag naggaar

No, you need a carpenter.

Ask: Do you know a good carpenter?

تعرف نجار كويس؟
teAraf naggaar kwayyis

3 minutes

لا، لازم واحد جديد. **laa laazim waaHid gideed** No, you need a new one.	ممكن تجيبه النهاردة؟ **mumkin tigeeboo innahaarda** Can you bring it today?	لا، حارجع بكرة الصبح. **laa HargaA bokra is-SubH** No, I'll come back tomorrow morning.

1 **WARM UP**

1 minute

Ask "**How do I get to the library?**" (pp.48–49).

How do you say "**cleaning staff**"? (pp.110–111).

Say "**It's 9:30**," "**10:45**," and "**12:00**" (pp.10–11 and pp.30–31).

Yeegee
TO COME

There are several ways of saying *come*. The word **gayy(a)** (*coming*) can be used with personal pronouns to mean *I'm coming*, *she's coming*, and so on. You need to add the ending **-een** for the plural (**gayyeen**). However, questions using **Aawiz(a)** or **mumkin** require the use of **agee** (*I come*) or **teegee** (*you come*).

2 **YEEGEE**: TO COME

6 minutes

Practice **yeegee** (*to come*) and the sample sentences, then test yourself using the cover flap.

أنا جاي/جاية **ana gayy/gayya**	I am coming (m/f)
أنت جاي **enta gayy**	you are coming (m)
أنت جاية **enti gayya**	you are coming (f)
هو جاي **howwa gayy**	he is coming
هي جاية **heyya gayya**	she is coming
احنا جايين **eHna gayyeen**	we are coming
أنتم جايين **entum gayyeen**	you are coming (pl)
هما جايين **humma gayyeen**	they are coming
ممكن أجي؟ **mumkin agee**	Can I come?
عاوز/عاوزة تيجي؟ **Aawiz/Aawza teegee**	Do you (m/f) want to come?

هما جايين بالقطر.
humma gayyeen bil-'aTr
They're coming by train.

Conversational tip In Arabic the word **gayy(a)** (*coming*) also means *next* as in *next week* or *next plane*—for example, **mumkin teegee il-usbooA ig-gayy?** (*can you come next week?*); **it-Tayyaara ig-gayya issaaAa kaam?** (*what time is the next plane?*); **hanzoor maSr essana ig-gayya** (*we'll visit Egypt next year*).

3 USEFUL PHRASES

4 minutes

Learn these phrases, then test yourself using the cover flap.

عامل/عاملة النضافة
بييجي / بتيجي كل يوم.
**Aaamil/Aaamilit naDafa
beyegee/beteegee kol yoom**
The cleaning staff (m/f)
comes every Monday.

When can I come?	ممكن أجي امتى؟ **mumkin agee imta**
Can you come on Sunday?	ممكن تيجي يوم الحد؟ **mumkin teegee yoom il-Had**
Are you (pl) coming tomorrow?	أنتم جايين بكرة؟ **entum gayyeen bokra**
Do you (m/f) want to come with us?	عاوز(ة) تيجي معانا؟ **Aawiz/-a teegee maAna**
Come! (to a man/ woman/group)	تعال (ي/وا) **taAaala/taAaalee/ taAaaloo**

4 PUT INTO PRACTICE

4 minutes

Complete this dialogue, then test yourself using the cover flap.

كوافير سوزي. أي خدمة؟
**kwafeer suzi.
ayyi khidma**

Suzi's hair salon.
Can I help you?

Say: I want an
appointment, please.

عاوزة ميعاد من فضلك.
Aawza miAaad min faDlik

عاوزة تيجي امتى؟
Aawza teegee imta

When do you
want to come?

Ask: Can I come today?

ممكن أجي النهاردة؟
**mumkin agee
innahaarda**

أيوه. الساعة كام؟
aywah. issaaAa kaam

Yes. What time?

Say: I want to
come at 10:30am.

عاوزة أجي عشرة ونص.
**Aawza agee Aashra
we nuS**

1 WARM UP

1 minute

What's the Arabic for **"big"** and **"small"**? (pp.64–65).

Say **"The room is big"** and **"The bed is small"** (pp.60–61, pp.64–65).

Il-shurTa wil-gareema
POLICE AND CRIME

If you are the victim of a crime while traveling or living in the MENA region, you will need to go to the police station to report it. Initially, you may have to explain your complaint in Arabic, so some basic vocabulary is useful.

2 **WORDS TO REMEMBER**: CRIME

4 minutes

Familiarize yourself with these words, then test yourself using the cover flap.

أنا عاوز محامي.
ana Aawiz muhaamee
I need a lawyer.

سرقة **sir'a**	burglary
محضر **maHDar**	police report
حرامي/حرامية **Haraamee/Haraamyya**	thief (m/f)
شرطي/شرطية **shurTee/shurTeyya**	police (m/f)
إفادة **efaada**	statement
شاهد/شاهدة **shahid/shahda**	witness (m/f)
محامي/محامية **muhaamee/ muhaamyya**	lawyer (m/f)

3 **USEFUL PHRASES**

3 minutes

Learn these phrases, then test yourself using the cover flap.

كاميرا
kamera
camera

محفظة
maHfaZa
purse

أنا اتسرقت. **ana itsara't**	I've been robbed.
سرقوا إيه؟ **sar'oo eh**	What was stolen?
شفت الفاعل؟ **shuft il-faaAil**	Did you see who did it?
السرقة حصلت امتى؟ **is-sir'a Hasalit imta**	When did the theft happen?

4 WORDS TO REMEMBER: APPEARANCE
5 minutes

Familiarize yourself with these words, then test yourself using the cover flap. Remember that adjectives have a feminine form ending in **-a**.

man	رجل **raagil**
woman	سيدة **sayyida**
tall, long (m/f)	طويل/طويلة **Taweel/Taweela**
short (m/f)	قصير/قصيرة **'uSayyar/'uSayyara**
young (m/f)	صغير/صغيرة **Sughayyar/Sughayyara**
old (m/f)	عجوز/عجوزة **Aagooz/Aagooza**
fat (m/f)	سمين/سمينة **sameen/sameena**
thin (m/f)	رفيع/رفيعة **rufayyaA/rufayyaAa**
his/her hair is long	شعره/شعرها طويل **shaAroo/shaAraha Taweel**
with glasses	بنظارة **bi-naDDaara**
beard	دقن **da'n**

هو قصير وبشنب.
howwa 'uSayyar wi bi-shanab
He is short, with a mustache.

شعره أسود وقصير.
shaAroo iswid wi-'uSayyar
His hair is black and short.

5 PUT INTO PRACTICE
2 minutes

Complete this dialogue, then test yourself using the cover flap.

كان شكله إيه؟
kaan shakloo eh
What was he like?
Say: Short and fat.
قصير وسمين. **'uSayyar wi-sameen**

وشعره؟
wi-shaAroo
And his hair?
Say: Long and black.
طويل وأسود. **Taweel wi iswid**

Cultural tip In Egypt, a special division of the Egyptian National Police Force called the Tourist and Antiquities Police are present at all important tourist sites. You can recognize them by their arm band, which states the name of the division.

RaagiA wi karrar
REVIEW AND REPEAT

To come

❶ جاي
gayy

❷ جايين
gayyeen

❸ أجي
agee

❹ جاية
gayya

❺ تيجي
teegee

1 TO COME

3 minutes

Fill in the blanks with the correct form of **yeegee** (*to come*).

❶ enta _____ bokra?

❷ humma _____ bil-'aTr

❸ (ana) mumkin _____ yoom is-sabt?

❹ heyya _____ il-usbooA ig-gayy

❺ enti Aawza _____ maAna?

Bank and mail

❶ طرد
Tard

❷ ظرف
zarf

❸ بطاقة بريدية
bitaa'a bareedyya

❹ كارت الائتمان
kart il-i'timaan

2 BANK AND MAIL

4 minutes

Name these items in Arabic.

❶ parcel

❷ envelope

credit card ❹

postcard ❸

SERVICES · 117

il-agweba *Answers*
(Cover with flap)

---

3   APPEARANCE

4 minutes

What do these sentences mean?

❶ **howwa taweel wi-rufayyaA**

❷ **shaAraha 'usayyar**

❸ **ir-raagil 'usayyar wi bi-naDDaara**

❹ **heyya Aagooza wi-sameena**

❺ **ana Taweel wi bi-shanab**

Appearance
❶ He is tall and thin.

❷ Her hair is short.

❸ The man is short, (and) he has glasses.

❹ She's old and fat.

❺ I am tall with a mustache.

---

4   THE PHARMACY

4 minutes

You are asking a pharmacist for advice. Join in the conversation, replying in Arabic following the numbered English prompts.

  ayyi khidma?
❶ I have a cough.

  Aandak bard kamaan?
❷ No, but I have a headache.

  Aandina Huboob
❸ Do you have this as a syrup?

  aywah. itfaDDal
❹ Thank you. How much is that?

  talaateen geneih
❺ Here you are. Goodbye.

The pharmacy
❶ عندي كحة.
Aandee koHHa

❷ لا، بس عندي صداع.
laa, bass Aandee sodaaA

❸ عندك ده دوا شُرب؟
Aandak dah dawa shorb

❹ شكرا. بكام ده؟
shukran. bikaam dah

❺ اتفضلي. مع السلامة.
itfaDDalee. maAa issalaama

Wa't il-faraagh
LEISURE TIME

The MENA region provides many opportunities for cultural pursuits and modern leisure activities. Be prepared for any of these to be the subject of conversation by using the terms on these pages. Note that **il** (*the*) usually follows *like, love, interested in,* and *prefer*: **bitHibb il-fann?** (*do you like art?*), but may or may not follow *fond of*: **howwa ghaawee/ heyya ghaawya qira'a** (*he's/she's fond of reading*).

1 WARM UP
1 minute

What is the Arabic for **"museum"** and **"art gallery"**? (pp.48–49).

Say **"I'm not fond of cats"** (pp.104–105).

Ask a woman **"Do you want…?"** (pp.24–25).

2 WORDS TO REMEMBER

Familiarize yourself with these words, then test yourself using the cover flap.

مسرح **masraH**	theater
موسيقى **mooseeqa**	music
فن **fann**	art
سينما **sinima**	cinema
ألعاب الفيديو **alAaab il-vidyoo**	video games
ملهى ليلي/نايت كلَب **malha laylee/nayt clab**	nightclub
رياضة **riyaaDa**	sports
زيارة المعالم **ziyaarit il-maAaalim**	sightseeing

راقص
raaqis
dancer

زي تقليدي
ziyy taqleedee
traditional costume

3 IN CONVERSATION

أهلاً رنا. تحبي تلعبي تنس النهاردة الصبح؟
ahlan Rana, teHebee telAabee tinis innahaarda eSSobHs

Hi Rana, do you want to play tennis this morning?

لا شكرًا، هعمل حاجة تانية.
laa, shukran haAmel Haga tanya

No thank you. I have other plans.

هتعملي إيه؟
hateamelee eh

Oh, what are you going to do?

5 SAY IT
2 minutes

I like music.

I prefer the theater.

I'm not fond of sports.

Shopping is boring!

أنا بأحب الرقص.
ana baHib ir-ra's
I like dancing.

4 🔊 USEFUL PHRASES
4 minutes

Learn these phrases, then test yourself using the cover flap.

What are your (m/f) interests?	هواياتك إيه؟ **hiwayaatak/-ik eh**
What do you (m/f) plan to do this morning?	هتعمل/هتعملي إيه النهاردة الصبح؟ **hateAmel/hateAmelee eh innahaarda essobH**
I like art.	أنا باحب الفن. **ana baHib il-fann**
I prefer the cinema.	أنا بأفضل السينما. **ana bafaDDal is-sinima**
I'm interested (m/f) in music.	أنا مهتم/مهتمة بالموسيقى. **ana mohtam/mohtamma bel-mooseeqa**
I'm fond (m/f) of the theater.	أنا غاوي/غاوية مسرح. **ana ghaawee/ghaawya masraH**
I hate shopping.	بكره التسوق. **bakrah il-tasawwoq**
That's boring.	ده ممل. **dah mumill**

بحب ألعاب الفيديو.
baHib alAaab il-vidyoo
I love video games.

4 minutes

هروح أزور المعالم السياحية. تيجي معايا؟ **harooH azoor ilmaAaalem issyaHeyya** I am going sightseeing! Do you want to join me?	فكرة حلوة, بس أنا هلعب تنس. **fekra Helwa, bass ana HalAab tinis** That sounds nice, but I want to play tennis.	مفيش مشكلة. حظ سعيد في المباراة. **mafeesh mushkila. Haz saAeed fel mubarah** No problem. Good luck with your game!

1 WARM UP

1 minute

Ask "**Do you (f) want to play tennis?**" (pp.118–119).

Say "**I like the theater**" and "**I prefer sightseeing**" (pp.118–119).

Say "**I'm not fond of art**" (pp.118–119).

Ir-riyaaDa wil-hiwaayaat
SPORTS AND HOBBIES

Soccer and diving are very popular in the MENA region, as are walking, running, cycling, tennis, and fishing. The verb **biyHibb** (*to like*) is useful for talking about sports and hobbies. The negative is made by using **ma-** as a prefix and **-(i)sh** as a suffix: **mabiyHibbish** (*he doesn't like*).

2 WORDS TO REMEMBER

4 minutes

Familiarize yourself with these words, then test yourself using the cover flap. Note the word **koora** (*ball, globe,* or *sphere*) is in the names of many sports: **koorat is-salla** (*ball of the basket*) and **koorat il-qadam** (*ball of the foot*). Soccer is often shortened to just **il-koora** (*the ball*).

كرة القدم **koorat il-qadam**	soccer
كرة السلة **koorat is-salla**	basketball
تنس **tinis**	tennis
السباحة **is-sibaaHa**	swimming
الإبحار **il-ibHaar**	sailing
صيد السمك **Seid is-samak**	fishing
ركوب العجلة **rokoob il-Aagala**	cycling
الجري **ig-garey**	running
ركوب الخيل **rokoob il-kheil**	horse riding

زعانف
zaAaanif
fins

تنك هواء
tank hawa
oxygen tank

نظارة بحر
naDDaarit baHr
mask

بدلة غطس
badlit ghaTs
wet suit

باحب الغطس جدا.
baHib il-ghaTs giddan
I like diving very much.

3 USEFUL PHRASES

3 minutes

Learn these phrases, then test yourself using the cover flap.

أنا باحب الكرة. **ana baHib il-koora**	I like soccer.
هي بتحب الجري. **heyya bitHibb ig-garey**	She likes running.
هو بيحب الصيد أوي. **howwa beyHib isseid awee**	He likes fishing very much.

4 BIYHIBB: TO LIKE

4 minutes

Practice **biyHibb** (*to like*) and the sample sentences, then test yourself using the cover flap.

I like (m/f)	(أنا) باحب	(ana) baHib
you like (m)	(أنا) بتحب	enta bitHibb
you like (f)	(أنت) بتحبي	enti bitHibbee
he likes	(هو) بيحب	(howwa) beyHib
she likes	(هي) بتحب	(heyya) bitHibb
we like	(إحنا) بنحب	(eHna) binHib
you like (pl)	(انتم) بتحبو	(entum) bitHiboo
they like	(همة) بيحب	(humma) biyHiboo

بتحب/بتحبي المراكب؟
bitHibb/bitHibbee il-maraakib
Do you like (m/f) boats?

What do you like (m) doing?	بتحب تعمل إيه؟	bitHibb teAmel eh
What do you like (f) doing?	بتحبي تعملي إيه؟	bitHibbee teAmelee eh
I don't like diving.	ما باحبش الغطس.	mabaHibbish il-ghaTs

5 PUT INTO PRACTICE

3 minutes

Complete this dialogue, then test yourself using the cover flap.

بتحب تعمل إيه؟
bitHibb teAmel eh
What do you like doing?
Say: I like tennis.

أنا باحب التنس.
ana baHib it-tinis

بتحب الكرة؟
bitHibb il-koora
Do you like soccer?
Say: No, I'm not fond of soccer.

لا، أنا مش غاوي كرة.
laa, ana mish ghaawee koora

وكرة السلة؟
wi-koorat-salla
And basketball?
Say: Yes, I like basketball very much.

أيوه، أنا باحب كرة السلة جدا.
aywah, baHib koorat is-salla giddan

Iz-ziyaaraat
SOCIALIZING

1 **WARM UP** 1 minute

Say "**my husband**" and "**my wife**" (pp.10–11).

How do you say "**lunch**" and "**dinner**" in Arabic? (pp.20–21).

Say "**Sorry, I'm busy**" (pp.32–33).

The idea of hospitality is deeply embedded in Arabic culture, and food and shelter are central to the notion. While living or traveling in the region, you can expect to receive numerous invitations from people you meet and, as eating together is a time-honored way of developing trust and building relationships, you are likely to be offered lavish amounts of food when you visit.

2 🔊 **USEFUL PHRASES**

Learn these phrases, then test yourself using the cover flap.

عاوزين نعزمكم على العشاء.
Aawzeen niAzimkum Aalal Asha
We'd like to invite you (pl) to dinner.

فاضيين يوم الخميس؟
faaDiyeen yoom il-khamees
Are you (pl) free on Thursday?

يوم ثاني، معلش.
yoom taani, maAlish
Perhaps another day.

صاحبة البيت
saHbit il-beit
hostess

الأكل لذيذ.
il-akl lazeez
The food is delicious.

3 🔊 **IN CONVERSATION**

عاوزين نعزمكم يوم الثلاثاء.
Aawzeen niAzimkum yoom it-talaat

We'd like to invite you on Tuesday.

آسفة، احنا مشغولين.
aasfa, eHna mash-ghooleen

I'm sorry, we're busy.

طيب والخميس؟
Tayyib wil-khamees

Okay. What about Thursday?

Cultural tip When you visit someone for the first time, it is usual to take chocolate or cake. Having seen their house, you can take a slightly more personal gift if invited again.

Deifa
guest

3 minutes

4 WORDS TO REMEMBER

2 minutes

Familiarize yourself with these words, then test yourself using the cover flap.

party	حفلة	**Hafla**
dinner party	حفلة عشا	**Haflat Asha**
reception	حفلة استقبال	**Haflat isti'baal**
invitation	عزومة	**Aozooma**

5 PUT INTO PRACTICE

3 minutes

Complete this dialogue, then test yourself using the cover flap.

عاوزين نعزمكم على العشاء بكرة.
Aawzeen niAzimkum Aalal Asha bokra
We'd like to invite you to dinner tomorrow.
Say: Tomorrow would be very good.

بكرة مناسب جدا.
bokra munaasib giddan

الساعة ثمانية كويس؟
issaaAa tamanya kwayyis
Is 8 o'clock OK?
Say: Yes. Thank you for the invitation.

أيوه، شكرا على العزومة.
aywah. shukran Aalal Aozooma

6 minutes

أيوه، الخميس مناسب جدا.
aywah, il-khamees munaasib giddan

Yes, Thursday would be very good.

لازم تيجي مع زوجك.
laazim teegee maAa zoogik

Be sure to bring your husband.

طبعا، شكرا على العزومة.
TabAan. shukran Aalal Aozooma

Of course. Thank you for the invitation.

RaagiA wi karrar
REVIEW AND REPEAT

il-agweba *Answers*
(Cover with flap)

Animals

❶ عصفور
Aasfoor

❷ أرنب
arnab

❸ حصان
Husaan

❹ سمكة
samaka

❺ كلب
kalb

❻ قطة
oTTa

1 ANIMALS

Name these animals in Arabic.

horse **❸**

❶ bird   rabbit **❷**

dog **❺**

❻ cat

Preferences

❶ هي مش غاوية غطس.
**heyya mish
ghaawya ghaTs**

❷ أنا بأفضل كرة السلة.
**ana bafaDDal koorat
is-salla**

❸ أنا غاوي/غاوية كورة.
**ana ghaawee/
ghaawya koora**

❹ هو غاوي تنس.
howwa ghaawee tinis

2 PREFERENCES

4 minutes

Say these sentences in Arabic:

❶ She's not fond of diving.
❷ I prefer basketball.
❸ I'm fond of soccer.
❹ He likes tennis.

❶

❷

❸

❹

il-agweba *Answers*
(Cover with flap)

3 minutes

4 fish

3 TO LIKE
4 minutes

Use the different forms of the verb **biyнibb** in these sentences.

1 ana _____ il-koora

2 howwa _____ is-sibaaнa

3 heyya _____ kura is-salla

4 enti _____ it-tinis?

5 enta _____ il-ghaтs?

To like
1 بأحب
baнib

2 بيحب
beyнib

3 بتحب
bitнibb

4 بتحبي
bitнibbee

5 بتحب
bitнibb

4 AN INVITATION
4 minutes

You are invited to dinner. Join in the conversation, replying in Arabic following the numbered English prompts.

faaдiyeen yoom il-khamees?
1 I'm sorry, we're busy.

тayyib. wis-sabt?
2 Saturday would be very good.

laazim teegee maдa zoogik
3 Of course. What time shall we come?

issaaдa waaнda we nus idduhr
4 That's good for me.

An invitation
1 آسفة، احنا مشغولين.
aasfa, eнna mash-ghooleen

2 السبت مناسب جدا.
is-sabt munaasib giddan

3 طبعا. نيجي الساعة كام؟
таbдaan. neegee issaaдa kaam

4 ده مناسب ليا.
da munaasib leyya

Reinforce and progress

Regular practice is the key to maintaining and advancing your language skills. In this section you will find a variety of suggestions for reinforcing and extending your knowledge of Arabic. Many involve returning to exercises in the book and extending their scope by using the dictionaries. Go back through the lessons in a different order, mix and match activities to make up your own daily 15-minute program, or focus on topics that are of particular relevance to your current needs.

1 WARM UP | **1 minute**

Say **"He is vegetarian"** (pp.14–15).

Say **"She is not from Egypt"** and **"I don't have a car"** (pp.14–15).

What is the Arabic for **"children"**? (pp.10–11).

Match, repeat, and extend
Remind yourself of words related to specific topics by returning to the Match and Repeat and Words to Remember exercises. Test yourself using the cover flap. Discover new words in that area by referring to the dictionary and menu guide.

Keep warmed up
Revisit the Warm Up boxes to remind yourself of key words and phrases. Make sure you work your way through all of them on a regular basis.

---

2 **MATCH AND REPEAT** | **5 minutes**

Match the numbered items to the list, then test yourself using the cover flap.

❶ سطح
satH

❷ شباك
shibbaak

❸ برجولة
bergoola

❹ بلكونة
balkoona

❺ سلالم
salaalim

❻ باب
baab

❼ حائط
HeiTa

❽ مدخل
madkhal

❶ roof ❷ window ❸ pergola ❹ balcony

stairs ❺ door ❻ ❼ wall ❽ driveway

Carry on conversing
Reread the In Conversation panels. Say both parts of the conversation, paying attention to the pronunciation. Where possible, try incorporating new words from the dictionary.

3 **IN CONVERSATION**

أهلاً، أنا أستاذة
هالة شوقي.
**ahlan, ana ustaaza
haala shawqi**

Hello, I'm Professor Hala Shawqi.

من أي جامعة؟
min ayyi gamAa

From which university?

من جامعة اسكندرية.
**min gamAit
iskendereyya**

From the University of Alexandria.

Practice words and phrases
Return to the Words to Remember, Useful Phrases, and Put into Practice exercises. Test yourself using the cover flap. When you are confident, devise your own versions of the phrases, using new words from the dictionary.

| 4 🔊 | **USEFUL PHRASES**: MONTHS | 2 minutes |

Learn these phrases, then test yourself using the cover flap.

My children have a holiday in August.

أولادي عندهم اجازة
في أغسطس.
uwlaadee Aanduhum
agaaza fi aghusTus

My birthday is in June.

عيد ميلادي في يونيو.
Aeed milaadee
fi yoonyo

| 5 | **SAY IT** 2 minutes |

I do research in medicine.
I have a degree in engineering.
Where's the lecture hall?

Say it again
The Say It exercises are a useful instant reminder for each lesson. Practice these using your own vocabulary variations from the dictionary or elsewhere in the lesson.

| 6 | **THIS IS MY...** | 4 minutes |

Say these sentences in Arabic.
❶ This is my wife.
❷ Is that her husband?
❸ That's our daughter.
❹ Is this your son?
  (talking to a man)

Review and repeat again
Work through a Review and Repeat lesson as a way of reinforcing words and phrases presented in the course. Return to the main lesson for any topic about which you are no longer confident.

Using other resources

As well as working with this book, try the following language extension ideas:

Visit Egypt, or another Arabic-speaking country, and try out your new skills with native speakers. Although this course focuses on Egyptian Arabic, you'll find this is widely understood by Arabic speakers from many regions.

Find out if there is an Arabic-speaking community near you. There may be shops, cafés, restaurants, or clubs. Try to visit some of these and use your Arabic to order food and drink and strike up conversations. Most native speakers will be happy to speak Arabic to you.

Join a language class or club. There are often evening and day classes available at a variety of different levels. Or you could start a club yourself if you have friends who are also interested in keeping up their Arabic.

Expand your knowledge of the Arabic script. Look at Arabic magazines and newspapers. The pictures will help you to understand the text. Look at the back of food packages and other products. You will often find a list of ingredients or components in Arabic. See if you can spot familiar letters and words and work out some other words by comparing them to the English equivalent.

Find language-learning websites, some of which will offer online help and activities, including games, tests, or even language exchanges.

Menu guide

This guide lists the most common terms you may encounter on Arabic menus or when shopping for food. The dishes are divided into categories, and the Arabic script is given to help you identify items on a menu. If you can't find an exact phrase, try looking up its component parts.

Essentials

بن	**bunn**	coffee, ground
دقيق	**di'ee'**	flour
بهارات	**buhaaraat**	herbs
مربى	**murabba**	jam
مكرونة	**makarona**	macaroni
مستردة	**mostarDa**	mustard
شعرية	**sheАreeya**	noodles (angel hair)
زيت	**zeit**	oil
فلفل أسود	**felfel iswid**	pepper, black
رُز	**ruz**	rice
ملح	**malН**	salt
مكرونة اسباجيتي	**makarona espagetti**	spaghetti
سكر	**sukkar**	sugar
شاي	**shaay**	tea
خل	**khall**	vinegar

Breads

عيش فينو	**Аeish feenoo**	baguette
خبز/عيش	**khobz/Аaysh**	bread
بقسماط	**bo'somaaT**	breadsticks
عيش سن	**Аeish sin**	brown bread, dry
عيش بلدي	**Аeish baladee**	brown bread, flat round
عيش كايزر	**Аeish kayzar**	buns
قُرص	**oraS**	buns, thin, sweet/salty
عيش محمص	**Аeish muНammaS**	crispbread
عيش شامي بني	**Аeish shaamee bonnee**	pita bread, brown
عيش شامي	**Аeish shaamee**	pita bread, white

Fruit and nuts

لوز	**looz**	almonds
تفاح	**tuffaaн**	apples
مشمش	**mishmish**	apricots
موز	**mooz**	bananas
توت	**toot**	berries
جوز هند	**gouz hind**	coconut
تين	**teen**	figs
جريب فروت	**greib froot**	grapefruit
عنب	**Aenab**	grapes
بندق	**bundu'**	hazelnuts
ليمون	**laymoon**	limes/lemons
منجة	**manga**	mangoes
شمام	**shammaam**	melon
برتقال	**borto'aan**	oranges
خوخ	**khookh**	peaches
فول سوداني	**fool soodaanee**	peanuts
كمثرى	**kommetra**	pears
أناناس	**anaanaas**	pineapple
فزدق	**fuzdu'**	pistachio nuts
برقوق	**bar'oo'**	plums
زبيب	**zibeeb**	raisins
فراولة	**farawla**	strawberries
يوستفندي	**yoostafandee**	tangerines
بطيخ	**baттeekh**	watermelon

Vegetables

خرشوف	**kharshoof**	artichokes
بنجر	**bangar**	beets
كرمب	**koronb**	cabbage
جزر	**gazar**	carrots
أرنبيط	**arnabeeт**	cauliflower
كرفس	**karafs**	celery
ذرة	**dorra**	corn
خيار	**khiyaar**	cucumber
باذنجان	**baadingaan**	eggplant
ثوم	**toom**	garlic
بصل أخضر	**baSal akhDar**	green onions
عدس	**Aads**	lentils
خس	**khass**	lettuce

بامية	fasoliya	navy beans
فاصوليا	baamya	okra
بصل	basal	onions
بسلة	bisilla	peas
بطاطس	baтaaтis	potatoes
فجل	figl	radishes
سبانخ	sabaanekh	spinach
بطاطا	baтaaтaa	sweet potatoes
طماطم	тamaaтem	tomatoes
لفت	lift	turnips
كوسة	koosa	zucchini

Meat and poultry

لحم بقري	lahm ba'aree	beef
روزبيف	rozbeef	beef, roast
فراخ / دجاج	firaakh/dajaaj	chicken
كستليتة / ريش	kosteleeta/reyash	cutlets
بط	batt	duck
اسكالوب	eskaalob	escalope
فيليتو	feeletto	fillet
لحم ضاني	laнm Daanee	lamb
شاورمة	shawerma	lamb/chicken, sliced and spit roasted
كبدة	kebda	liver
لحم	laнm	meat
لحم مفروم	laнm mafroom	meat, minced
كفتة	kofta	meat, minced or in balls, grilled on a skewer
كباب	kabaab	meat (usually lamb), cubed and grilled on a skewer
مشويات مشكلة	mashweeyaat mishakkila	mixed grill
حمام	нamaam	pigeon
سجق	sogo'	sausages
ديك رومي	deek roomee	turkey
بتلو	bitilloo	veal

Fish

أنشوجة	**anshooga**	anchovies
كابوريا	**kaaboriya**	crab
تعبان البحر	**tiAbaan il-bahr**	eel
سمك	**samak**	fish
سمك مقلي	**samak ma'lee**	fish, fried
سمك مشوي	**samak mashwee**	fish, grilled
سمك صيادية	**samak sayyadeeya**	fish with rice
استاكوزا	**estakooza**	lobster
سمك بوري	**samak booree**	mullet
اخطبوط	**akhtaboot**	octopus
سردين	**sardeen**	sardines
قاروص	**aroos**	sea bass
جمبري	**gambaree**	shrimp
سمك موسى	**samak moosa**	sole
سبيط	**subbeiT**	squid
تونة	**toona**	tuna

Eggs and dairy

زبدة	**zibda**	butter
جبن/جبنة	**gibn/gibna**	cheese
جبنة رومي	**gibna roomee**	cheese, hard
جبنة قديمة	**gibna adeema**	cheese, mature
مش	**mish**	cheese, salty
جبنة فلاحي	**gibna fallaahee**	cheese, soft farmer's
جبنة بيضاء	**gibna beiDa**	cheese, white
بيض	**beiD**	eggs
بيض مسلوق	**beiD masloo'**	eggs, boiled
بيض مقلي	**beiD ma'le**	eggs, fried
شكشوكة	**shakshooka**	eggs, scrambled with minced meat
حليب/لبن	**Haleeb/laban**	milk
أومليت	**omlet**	omelet
عجة	**Aegga**	omelet with onions and parsley
زبادي	**zabaadee**	yogurt
لبنة	**labna**	yogurt, strained

Starters, soups, and salads

جرجير	**gargeer**	arugula
حمص	**Hummus**	hummus–cooked and blended chickpeas
بطارخ	**baTaarikh**	mullet roe
زيتون	**zaytoon**	olives
مخلل	**mekhallil**	pickles
سلطة	**salaTa**	salad
سلطة باذنجان	**salaTit baadingaan**	salad, eggplant
سلطة بلدي	**salaTa baladee**	salad, Egyptian
سلطة خضراء	**salaTa khaDra**	salad, green
سلطة بطاطس	**salatit baTaaTis**	salad, potato
سلطة طماطم	**salaatit TamaaTem**	salad, tomato
سلطة زبادي	**salaatit zabaadee**	salad, yogurt
ساندوتش	**sandawitsh**	sandwich
سردين	**sardeen**	sardines
شوربة	**shorba**	soup
شوربة فراخ	**shorbit firaakh**	soup, chicken
شوربة سمك	**shorbit samak**	soup, fish
شوربة عدس	**shorbit Aads**	soup, lentil
شوربة خضار	**shorbit khuDaar**	soup, vegetable
تبولة	**tabboola**	tabbouleh–salad with bulgur, parsley, cucumber, and tomato
طحينة	**TaHeena**	tahini–sesame seed paste
بابا غنوج	**baaba ghannoog**	tahini with eggplant
ورق عنب	**wara' Aenab**	vine leaves, stuffed

Traditional Arabic dishes

طاجن	**Taagin**	casserole
كسكس بالضاني	**kuskus biDDaanee**	couscous–lamb and steamed semolina
مكدوس	**makdoos**	eggplant, oil-cured
مسقعة	**mesa'aAa**	eggplant with minced meat
فلافل/طعمية	**falaafel/taAmyya**	falafel–deep-fried balls of ground beans or chickpeas
فول بالزيت	**fool bizzeit**	fava beans, mashed with oil

كباب سمك	**kabaab samak**	grilled fish on a skewer
منسف	**mansaf**	lamb cooked in a sauce of fermented dried yogurt and served with rice or bulgur
مندى	**mandee**	meat/chicken and rice with special spices
بسلة باللحمة	**bisilla bil-laнma**	meat cooked with peas
طاجن بامية	**таagin bamya**	okra stew
صفيحة	**sefeeнa**	pastry base topped with minced lamb
حواوشي	**hawawshi**	pita bread, stuffed
كشري	**kosharee**	rice, lentils, pasta, and onions with a piquant sauce
فتة	**fatta**	rice with bread and meat
ملوخية بالفراخ	**molookheeya bil-firaakh**	soup of greens with chicken
تورلي	**torli**	vegetable stew
محشي	**maнshee**	vegetables, stuffed

Desserts

بقلاوة/ جُلاش	**ba'laawa/gollash**	baklava–pastry, fine-layered with nuts in syrup
قراقيش	**ara'eesh**	biscuits, sometimes stuffed with dates
معمول	**maдmool**	cake stuffed with dates
قشطة	**ishta**	cream, thick
كريم كرامل	**krem karamel**	crème caramel
الحلو	**il-нelew**	dessert
خشاف	**khoshaaf**	fruits, stewed
سلطة فواكه	**salaтit fawaakih**	fruit salad
عسل	**дasal**	honey
آيس كريم	**ays kreem**	ice cream
أم علي	**umm дalee**	"Mother of Ali" – pudding with raisins and milk

كنافة	**kunaafa**	pastry, angel hair, with nuts in syrup
دنش	**danash**	pastry, Danish
فطير	**feTeer**	pastry, layered with ghee or butter, sweet/salty
رز بلبن	**ruz bi-laban**	rice pudding
بسبوسة	**basboosa**	semolina cake with syrup
ملبن	**malban**	Turkish delight

Drinks

بيرة	**beera**	beer
قهوة	**ahwa**	coffee
قهوة بدون حليب	**ahwa bidoon Haleeb**	coffee, black
قهوة مضبوط	**ahwa mazboot**	coffee, medium sweet
قهوة زيادة	**ahwa ziyaada**	coffee, very sweet
قهوة بالحليب	**ahwa bi-Haleeb**	coffee, with milk
قهوة سادة	**ahwa saada**	coffee, without sugar
كولا	**cola**	cola
عصير فواكه	**Aaseer fawaakih**	juice, fruit
عصير جوافة	**Aaseer gawaafa**	juice, guava
عصير ليمون	**Aaseer laymoon**	juice, lemon
عصير منجة	**Aaseer manga**	juice, mango
عصير برتقال	**Aaseer borto'aan**	juice, orange
عصير طماطم	**Aaseer TamaaTim**	juice, tomato
عصير فراولة	**Aaseer farawla**	juice, strawberry
عصير قصب	**Aaseer asab**	juice, sugar cane
تمر هندي	**tamr hindi**	tamarind drink
شاي	**shaay**	tea
شاي بدون حليب	**shaay bidoon Haleeb**	tea, black

كركديه	**karkadeih**	tea, hibiscus
شاي بحليب	**shaay bi-Haleeb**	tea, with milk
شاي مع نعناع	**shaay maA naAnaaA**	tea, mint
مياه	**mayya**	water
مياه معدنية	**mayya maAdaneyya**	water, mineral
صودا	**sooda**	water, soda
نبيذ	**nibeedh**	wine
نبيذ أبيض	**nibeedh abyaD**	wine, white
نبيذ أحمر	**nibeedh aHmar**	wine, red

Methods of preparation

في الفرن	**fil-furn**	baked
مشوي على الفحم	**mashwee Aalal-faHm**	barbecued
مسلوق	**masloo'**	boiled
بالصلصة	**bis-salsa**	cooked in tomato sauce
محمر	**muHammar**	deep-fried
مقلي	**ma'lee**	fried
مشوي	**mashwee**	grilled
محشي	**maHshee**	stuffed

Dictionary
ENGLISH TO ARABIC

This dictionary contains the vocabulary from this book, together with many other frequently used words. You can find additional terms for food and drink in the Menu Guide (pp.128–135). Arabic adjectives (adj) vary according to the gender of the word they describe and whether it is singular or plural. In general, you can add **-a** to refer to the feminine singular and the plural of objects and adjectives. The most common ending for the plural of words that refer to people is **-een**. Verbs (verb) are shown in the masculine singular form of the present tense.

A

about (approximately) **Hawaalee**
accelerator **dawaasit il-banzeen**
accepted (adj) **ma'bool**
accident **Hadsa**
accommodation **maskan**
accountant **muHaasib**
ache **alam, wagaA**
adaptor (electrical) **tawseela**
address **Ainwaan**
admission charge **rasm id-dukhool**
after **baAd**
afternoon **baAd iD-Duhr**
aftershave **koloniyit baAd ilHilaa'a**
again **marra tanya, taanee**
against **Didd**
agent (realtor) **simsaar**
air-conditioning **takyeef**
air freshener **muaTTir hawa**
air hostess **muDeefa gaweyya**
air mail **bareed gawwee**
aircraft **Tayyaara**
airline **khaTT Tayaraan**
airport **maTaar**
alarm clock **menabbih**
alcohol **koHol**
Algeria **il-gazaa'ir**
all **kull, gameeA**;
  all the streets **kull ish-shawaariA**
allergy **Hassaaseyya**
allowed **masmooH**
almost **ta'reeban**
also **kamaan**
always **dayman**
am: I am **ana**
ambulance **isAaaf**

America **amreeka**
American (man) **amreekaanee**; (woman) **amreekaaneyya**; (adj) **amreekaanee**
Ancient Egypt **masr il-'adeema**
Ancient Egyptians **qodamaa' il-masreyyeen**
and **wi**
animal **Haywaan**
ankle **kaaHel**
another (adj) (different) **taanee**; (additional) **iDaafee**
answering machine **ansar masheen, rad 'aalee**
antique shop **maHal anteekaat**
antiseptic **moTahher**
apartment (flat) **sha'a**
apartment block **Aomaara**
appetite **shaheyya**
apples **tofaaH**
application form **istimaara**
appointment **miAaad**
apricot **mishmish**
April **abreel**
architect's drawings **rusoomaat handaseyya**
architecture **il-miAmaar**
are: you are (masculine) **enta**; (feminine) **enti**; (plural) **entum**; we are **eHna**; they are **humma**
area (region) **manti'a**
arm **diraaA**
armchair **kursee bemasaaned lil deraaAeen**
around **Hawl**
arrivals (airport, etc) **wusool**
arrive (verb) **yowsal**
art **fann**

art gallery **matHaf fonoon**
artist **fannaan**
arts (subject of study) **il-aadaab**
ashtray **menfaDit sagaayir**
asleep (adj) **naayim**; he's asleep **huwwa naayim**
asthma **rabwu**
at: at the post office **fi maktab il-bareed**; at night **bil-leil**; at 3 o'clock **is-saAa talaata**; at the roundabout **Aand id-dawaraan**
ATM **makanit eh tee im**
attractive (adj) **gazzaab**
August **aghusTus**
aunt (maternal) **khaala**; (paternal) **Amma**
Australia **ostoraalya**
Australian (man) **ostoraalee**; (woman) **ostoraaleyya**; (adj) **ostoraalee**
Austria **in-nemsa**
automatic (adj) **otomaateeki**
away: far away (adj) **baAeed**; go away! **imshee!**
awful (adj) **weHish giddan**
axe **balTa**
axle **il faas**

B

baby **Tifl, raDeea**
baby wipes **waraa'il aTfaal**
back (not front) **wara**; (body) **Dahr**
bad (adj) **weHesh, radee'**
bag **kees, shanTa**
baggage check-in **tasgeel elshonaT**
Bahrain **il-baHrein**
bait **TuAm**
bake (verb) **yikhbiz**
baker **khabbaaz**

bakery **makhbaz**

balcony **balkoona**

ball **koora**

ballpoint pen **alam gaaf**

banana **mooza, mooz**

band (musicians) **fir'a**

bandage **robaaт**

bank **bank**

barbecued (adj) **mashwee Alal faнm**

barber **нallaa'**

basement **badroom**

basin (sink) **нooD**

basket **salla**

basketball **koorat is-salla**

bath **banyo**; to have a bath (verb) **yistaнamma**

bathrobe **roob нammaam**

bathroom **нammaam**

bathtub **banyo**

battery **baттaareyya**

boarding gate **bawwaaba**

bazaar **bazaar, soo'**

be (verb) **yikoon: ana/eнna** (m/f/pl); I was... **ana kunt...**; he was... **howwa kaan...**; she was... **heyya kaanit...**; it was... **kaan...**

beach **shaaтi'**

beans **fool**

beard **liнya**

beautiful (adj) **gameel**

beauty products **muntagaat tagmeel**

because **Alashaan**

bed **sireer**

bed linen **melaayaat is-sireer**

bedroom **ghurfit noom**

beef **laнm ba'aree**

beer **beera**

before **abl**

beginner (adj) **mubtadi'**

behind **wara, khalf**

beige (adj) **beij**

bell **garas**

belly dance **ra's baladee**

below **taнт, asfal**

belt **нizaam**

beside **ganb, bi-gaanib**

best (adj) **aнsan, afDal**

better (adj) **aнsan**

between **bayn**

bicycle **Aagala, darraaga**

big (adj) **kibeer**

bikini **mayoh bekeenee**

bill **нisaab, fatoora**

bird **Aasfoor**

birthday **Aeed milaad**; happy birthday! **Aeed milaad saAeed!** birthday present **hadeeyit Aeed milaad**

biscuit **baskaweet**

bite (verb) **yiAoDD**; (noun) **aDDa**; (by insect) **ladgha**

bitter (adj) **murr**

black (adj) **iswid/sooda**

blanket **baттanyya**

blind (adj) (cannot see) **kafeef**

blinds **sitaara**

blinker (car) **ishaara**

blister **fa'foo'a**

blood **dam**; blood test **taнleel dam**

blouse **bilooza**

blue (adj) (m/f) **azra'/zar'a**

boarding pass **kart suAood**

boat **markib**; (rowing) **qaareb**

body **gism**

boil (verb) **yighlee**

boiled (adj) **masloo'**

bolt (noun: on door) **terbaas**

bones **AaDm**

book (noun) **kitaab**; (verb) **yiнgiz**

booking office **maktab il-нagz**

bookshop **maktaba**

boot (footwear) **boot**

border **нudood**

boring (adj) **mumill**

horn: I was born in...; **ana mawlood fi...**

bottle **izaaza**

bottle opener **fattaaнit azaayiz**

bottom (of sea, box, etc) **qaA**

bowl (dog) **таba' akl lil kalb**

box **sundoo'**

boy **walad**

boys **awlaad**

bra **sutyaan**

bracelet **eswera**

brakes (noun) **faraamil**

branch **farA**

brass **naнaas**

bread **Aeish, khubz**

breakdown (car) **Aarabeyya Aтlaana**; (nervous) **inhiyaar Aasabee**

breakfast **fiтaar, fuтoor**

breathe (verb) **yitnaffis**; I can't breathe **mish aa'dir atnaffis**

bricklayer **banna**

bridge **kubree, jisr**

briefcase **shanтa**

British (adj) **briтaanee**

broken (adj) **maksoor, baayiz**; broken leg **rigl maksoora**

brooch **brosh**

brother **akh**

brown (adj) **bunnee**

bruise **kadma**

brush (for sweeping) **meknasa**; (paint, tooth) **fursha**

bucket **gardal**

budget (noun) **mizaaneyya**

builder **bannaa**

building **mabnaa**

bumper **iksiDaam**

burglar **lis**

burn (verb) **yiнra'**; (noun) **нar'**

bus **otobees, baas, нaafila**

bus station **манаттit il-otobees**

bus stop **mawqaf otobees**

business **AAmaal**

business card **kart shakhsee**

businessman **raagil AAmaal**

businesswoman **sayyidit AAmaal**

busy (adj) (occupied) **mashghool**; (street) **zaнma**

but **bass, laakin**

butcher **gazzaar**

butter **zibda**

button **zoraar**

buy (verb) **yishtiri**

by: by the window **ganb bi-gaanib ish-shibaak**; by myself **waнdee**

C

cabbage **kurunb**

café **ahwa, maqha**

cake **torta, keika**

cake shop **нalawaanee**

calculator **aala нaasba**

calendar (agenda) **ajenda**

call: what's it called? **ismuh/ismaha eh?**

camel **gamal**

camera **kamera**

campsite **muAaskar**

can: can I have ...? **mumkin...?**

can (tin) **Ailba**

can opener **fattaaнit Ailab**

Canada **kanada**
Canadian (man) **kanadee**;
   (woman) **kanadeyya**;
   (adj) **kanadee**
cancer **saraTaan**
candle **shamAa**
canoe **kaanoo**
cap (bottle) **ghaTaa'**; (hat)
   caab
car **Aarabyya**
car seat (for a baby)
   kursee aTfaal
caravan **karavaan**
carburetor **kabrateir**
card **kart**
careful: be careful! **khalli**
   baalak!
carpenter **naggaar**
carpet **siggaada**
carriage (train) **Aaraba**
carrot **gazar**
case (suitcase) **shanTa**
cash **fuloos, kaash**, **naqdan**;
   (coins) **fakka**; to pay cash
   yidfaA kaash, yidfaA
   naqdan
cashier **sarraaf**
castle **alAa**
cat **oTTa**
catacombs **saraadeeb**
cathedral **kaatedraa'eyya**
cauliflower **arnabeeT**
cave **kahf**
CD **seedee**
ceiling **sa'f**
cemetery **ma'bara**
center **markaz**; town center
   wesT il-balad
certainly **Haadir**
certificate **shahaada**
chair **kursee**
chandelier **qandeel**
change (noun: money)
   fakka; (verb: money)
   yisrif; (verb: trains,
   clothes) **yighayyar**
charger (for phone, etc)
   shaaHin
charging cable **kabl**
   esh-shaHn
charging point/station (for
   car) **maHaTTit shaHn**
   sayyaraat
cheap (adj) **rekhees**
check-in **tasgeel al-wusool**
check-out **il-mughaadra**
cheers! (health) **fi**
   siHHitak!
cheese **gibna, jubn**
chef **sheef, Tabbaakh**

check **sheek**
checkbook **daftar**
   sheekaat
cherry **kereez**
chess **shaTarang**
chessboard **lawHit ish**
   shaTarang
chest (anatomical)
   sidr
chest of drawers
   magmooAet adraag
chewing gum **lebaan**
chicken **firaakh, dajaaj**
child **Tifl**
children **awlaad**,
   aTfaal
chimney **madkhana**
China **is-seen**
Chinese (man) **seenee**;
   (woman) **seeneyya**; (adj)
   seenee
chips **baTaaTis shibsee**
chocolate **shokolaata**; box
   of chocolates **Ailbit**
   shokolaata
church **kaneesa**
cigar **sigaar**
cigarette kiosk **koshk**
   sagaayir
cigarettes **sagaayir**
cinema **sinima**
city **madeena, balad**
city center **wesT il-balad**,
   wesT il-madeena
class (school) **fasl**; first class
   daraga oola; second
   class **daraga tanya**
classical Arabic **il-fus-Ha**
classical music **mooseeqa**,
   klaaseekeyya
clean (adj) **niDeef**;
   (verb) **yinaDDaf**
cleaning staff **Aaamil/**
   Aaamilit naDafa
clear (adj) (obvious)
   waaDiH; (water)
   safee; is that
   clear? **dah waaDiH?**
clever (adj) **shaaTir**
client **Aameel**
clock **menabbih, saaAa**
close (adj) (not open)
   ma'fool; the shop is
   closed **il-maHal ma'fool**;
   (near) **urrayyib**; (stuffy)
   katma; (verb) **yi'fil**
clothes **malaabis**
club **naadi**; (cards)
   sebaatee
clutch **debriyaaj**

coach (bus) **otobees, baas**;
   (of train) **Arabeyyit**
   il-'aTr
coach station **maHaTTit**
   il-otobees
coat **balTo**
coat hanger **shammaaAa**
cockroach **sorsaar**
coffee **ahwa**
coffee pot **kanaka**
coin **Aumla**
cold (illness) **bard**;
   (adj) **baarid**
collar **yaa'a**; (dog) **Too'**
   il-kalb
collection (stamps, etc)
   magmooAa
color **loon**
color film **film alwaan**
comb (noun) **meshT**;
   (verb) **yimashshaT**
come/coming (verb)
   yeegee: (m/f/pl) **gayy/**
   gayya/gayyeen; we
   came last week **gayna**
   il-usbooA illi faat; come!
   (m/f/pl) **taAaala!/**
   taAaalee!/taAaaloo!; I
   come from... **ana min...**
company (business)
   sherka
complicated (adj)
   muAaqqad
computer **kombyootar**
computer games **alAaab**
   il-kombyootar
concert **Hafla**
   mooseeqeyya
conditioner (hair) **balsam**
   shaAr
conductor (bus) **komsaree**;
   (orchestra) **qaa'ed**
   il-orkestra
conference **mu'tamar**
congratulations! **mabrook!**
constipation **imsaak**
consulate **unsuleyya**
contact lenses **Adasaat**
   laasiqa
contact solution (for
   contact lenses); **maHlool**
   lil-Adasaat il-laasiqa
contactless payment
   becart waiy faiy
contraceptive **maaniA lil**
   Haml
contract **Aa'd**
cook (noun) **Tabbaakh**;
   (verb) **yuTbukh**
cool (adj) **baarid**

copier (photocopier)
  makanit tasweer
copper **naнaas**
cork **fell**
corkscrew **barreema**
corner **rukn**; (street) **nasya**
corridor **mamarr**
cosmetics **mustaнDaraat**
  tagmeel
cost (verb) **yitkallif**; what
  does it cost? **bi-kaam dah?**
cot **sireer aтfaal**
cotton **uтn**
cotton wool **uтn тibbee**
cough (verb) **yikoнн, yisлal**;
  (noun) **коннa, soдaal**
countertop **saтh**
  il-maтbakh
country (state) **dawla**;
  (not town) **reef**
course (dish) **тaba'**; main
  course **iт-тaba' ir-ra'eesee**
cousin (male) (paternal) **ibn**
  лamm/лamma; (maternal)
  ibn khaal/khaala; (female)
  (paternal) **bint лamm**
  лamma; (maternal) **bint**
  khaal/khaala
cow **ba'ara**
crab **kaboria**
cramp **taqallos**
  il-aдalaat
cream **kreem**
credit card **kart/biтaa'it**
  il-i'timaan
crew **тaaqem**
crime **gareema**
crowded (adj) **zaнma**
cruise **riнla baнreyya**
crutches **лokkaaz**
cry (verb) (weep) **yibkee**;
  (shout) **yiseeн**
cucumber **khiyaar**
cup **fingaan**
cupboard **doolaab**
curtains **sataayir**
cushion **khudadyya**
customs **gamaarik**
cut (noun) **aтa**; (verb)
  yi'тaa, yi'uss
cycling **rokoob il-лagala**

D

dad **baba**
dairy (shop) **labbaan**
dairy products
  muntagaat albaan
damp **reтooba**
dance/dancing (verb) **ra's**

dangerous (adj) **khaтar**
dark (adj) **Dalma, meдallim**
daughter **bint, ibna**
day **yoom**
dead (adj) **mayyit**
deaf (adj) **aтrash**
dear (adj) (person) **лazeez**;
  (expensive) **ghaalee**
debit card **kart viza**
December **disamber**
deck chair **kursee**
  blaaj
decorator **naqqaash**
deep (adj) **лameeq**
degree (university)
  shihaada
deliberately **лamdan**
delicious (adj) **lazeez**
delivery **tasleem**
dentist **doktoor/**
  тabeeb asnaan
dentures **тaqm asnaan**
deny (verb) **yinkir**
deodorant **mozeel лraq**
department **qism**
departure **raнeel**
departures (airport, etc)
  mughadra
desert **saнraa'**
designer **musammim**
dessert **il-нelew**
diabetes **(maraд) is-sukkar**
diamond (jewel) **il-maas**;
  (cards) **samboosak**
diaper **нaffaдaat**
diarrhea **ishaal**
dictionary **qaamoos**
die (verb) **yimoot**
diesel **deezil**
different (adj) **mukhtalif**;
  that's different **dah**
  mukhtalif
difficult (adj) **saab**
dining car **arabeyyit**
  il-maтaam
dining room **ghurfit**
  sufra/it-тaдaam
dining table **sufra**
dinner **лsha**
dinner party **нaflat лsha**
direction **ittigaah**
directory (telephone)
  daleel
dirty (adj) **qazer**
disabled (adj) **muдaqeen**,
  лagaza
dishes (on a menu)
  aтbaaq
dish soap **masноo'**
  aтbaa'

dishwasher **ghasaalit**
  il-aтbaa'
disposable diapers
  нaffaдaat
dive (verb) **yighтas**
dive boat **markib ghaтs**
diving **ghaтs**; diving gear
  лiddit ghaтs
diving board **menassit**
  il-ghaтs
divorced (adj) (man)
  muтallaq; (woman)
  muтallaqa
do (verb) **yeдmel**
doctor **doktoor, тabeeb**
document **mustanad**
dog **kalb**
doll **лroosa**
dollar **dolaar**
donkey **нumaar**
door **baab**
double room **ghurfa**
  li-shakhsein
down **asfal**
drawer **dorg**
drawing pin **dabboos**
  rasm
dress **fustaan**
drink (noun) **mashroob**;
  (verb) **yishrab**; would you
  like a drink? **tishrab(ee)**
  нaaga?
drinking water **mayyit**
  shurb
drive (verb) **yisoo'**
driver **sawwaa'**
driving license **rukhsa**
driveway **madkhal**
drops **nu'aт**
drunk (adj) **sakraan**
dry (adj) **gaaf**
dry cleaner **maнal**
  tanдeef
during **khilaal**
duster **minfaдa**
duty-free (adj) **aswaa'**
  нorra

E

each (every) **kull**; twenty
  pounds each **kull waaнid**
  bi-лishreen gineih
ear **uzun, widn**
early (adj) **badree,**
  mubakkir
earbuds **sammaдaat**
earrings **нala'**
east **sharq**
easy **sahl**

eat (verb) **yaakul**
editor **muнarrir**
eggs **beiD**
Egypt **masr**
eight **tamanya**
either: either of them **ayy minhum;** either... or **ya'ima... aw...**
elastic band **astik**
elbow **kooA**
electric (adj) **bik-kahrabaa**
electrician **kahrabaa'ee**
electricity **kahrabaa**
elevator **asansei**
else: something/anything else **Haaga tanya;** someone else **waaHid taanee;** somewhere else **makaan taanee**
email **email**
email address **Aenwaan il-eemail**
embarrassed (adj) **maksoof**
embassy **sifaara**
embroidery **taтreez**
emerald **zumorrod**
emergency **тawaari'**
Emirates **il-imaaraat**
employee **muwazzaf**
empty (adj) **faaDee**
end **nihaaya;** (adj) (last) **aakhir**
engaged (adj) (couple) **makhтoobeen;** (occupied) **mashghool**
engine (motor) **motoor, muнarrik**
engineer **muhandes**
engineering **handasa**
England **ingeltera**
English (adj) **ingleezee;** (language) **ingleezee**
Englishman **ingleezee**
Englishwoman **ingleezeyya**
enlargement **takbeer**
enough **kifaaya**
entertainment **tasleyya**
entrance **dukhool, madkhal**
entrance tickets **tazaakir id-dukhool**
envelope **zarf, mazroof**
epilepsy **saraA**
equipment **Aidda**
eraser **asteeka**
escalator **sillim bik kahrabaa**
especially **makhsooS**
estimate **elmablagh el-taqdeeree**

evening **masaa**
every **kull**
everyone **kulliwaaнid**
everything **kulliнaaga**
everywhere **kullimakaan**
example **misaal;** for example **masalan**
excellent (adj) **mumtaaz**
excess baggage **wazn zaayed**
exchange (verb) **yibaadil**
exchange rate **siAr is-sarf**
excursion **nuzha**
excuse me! (to get attention) **law samaнt!**
exhaust **Aadem (sayyarat)**
exhibition **maAraD**
exit **makhrag**
expensive (adj) **ghaalee**
experienced (adj) **shaaтir, khibra**
extension **tamdeed**
eye **Aein;** eyes (two) **Aeinein;** eyes (more than two) **Aoyoon**
eye drops **nu'aт lil-Aein**
eye glasses **naDaara**
eyebrow **нaagib**

F

face **wish, wajh**
face masks **kimamaat**
facilities (equipment, etc) **maraafiq**
faint (adj) (unclear) **baahit;** I feel faint **нasis biDaaf**
fair (funfair) **malaahee;** (adj) (just) it's not fair **dah mish Aadil**
false teeth **тa'm asnaan**
family **usra, Aela;** my family **usritee; Aeltee**
fan (ventilator) **marwaнa;** (enthusiast) **muAgab**
fan belt **seir il-marwaнa**
far (adj) **biAeed;** how far is it? **il-masaafa adda eh?**
fare **ogrit is-safar**
farm **mazraAa**
farmer **muzaariA**
fashion **il-mooDa**
fast (adj) **sareeA;** (noun: during Ramadan, etc) **soom**
fat (adj) (of person) **sameen, badeen;** (on meat, etc) **dihn**
father **ab, waalid**

father-in-law **нama**
February **febraayir**
feel (verb) (touch) **yilmis;** I feel hot **ana нarraan**
ferry **meAadeyya**
fever **нaraara**
fiancé **khaтeeb**
fiancée **khaтeeba**
field (of study) **magaal;** (meadows) **meroog**
fig **teen**
figures **arqaam**
filling (tooth) **нashow**
film **film**
filter **filtar**
finger **sobaaA**
fire **naar;** (blaze) **нaree'a**
fire extinguisher **тaffaayit нaree'**
fireworks **sawareekh**
first (adj) **awwal;** first aid **isAaafaat awwaleyya;** first floor **id-door il-awwal**
fish (singular) **samaka;** (plural, food) **samak**
fishing **seid is-samak;** fishing gear **Aiddit seid**
fishing boat **markib seid**
fishing rod **sinnaara**
fishmonger **maнal samak**
five **khamsa**
fizzy (adj) **fawwaar**
flag **Aalam**
flash (camera) **flaash**
flashlight **misbaaн yadawee**
flat (adj) (level) **musaттah**
flavor **тaAm**
flea **barghoot**
flight **riнlit тayaraan**
flip-flops **shibshib**
flippers **zAaanif**
floor (of room) **arDeyya**
flour **di'ee'**
flowers **ward, zuhoor**
flu **infilwanza**
fly (verb) **yiтeer;** (insect) **debaana**
fog **Dabaab**
folk music **mooseeqa shaAbeyya**
food **akl, тaAaam**
food poisoning **tasammum**
food stands **Aarabiyat Akl**
foot **qadam**
fond of (adj) **ghaawi**
for **Aalashaan, li;** for me **Aalashaanee;** what for? **leh?;** for a week **li-muddit usbooA**

foreigner (adj)
  agnabee
forest **ghaaba**
fork **shooka**
fortnight **usbooAein**
fountain pen **alam hibr**
four **arbaAa**
fourth (adj) **ir-raabiA**
fracture **kasr**
France **faransa**
free (of) (adj) **khaali** (min);
  (no cost) **maggaani**;
  (available) **faaDi**
freezer **freezar**
French (adj) **faransee**
french fries **baTaaTis**
  muHamarra
Friday **(yoom) il-gumAa**
fridge **tallaaga**
fried (adj) **ma'lee**
friend **saaHib, sadeeq**
friendly (adj) **laTeef**; (tame)
  aleef
front: in front of
  udaam, amaam
frost **saqeeA**
frozen products **muntagaat**
  mugammada
fruit **fawaakih**
fruit juice **Aaseer**
  fawaakih
fry (verb) **i'lee**
frying pan **Taasit il-alee**
full (adj) **malyaan**; *I'm full*
  ana shabAaan
full board **iqaama kamla**
funnel (for pouring) **qumA**
funny (adj) **muDHik;** (odd)
  ghareeb
furnished (adj) **mafroosh**
furniture **athaath**

G

garage **garaaj**
garden **gineina,**
  Hadeeqa
gardener **ganaaynee**
garlic **toom**
gas (petrol) **banzeen**
gas station
  maHaTTit banzeen
gear (equipment) **Aidda**
gearbox **fetees**
German (adj) **almaanee**
Germany **almaanya**
get (verb) (fetch) **yigeeb;**
  have you got...? **Andak/**
  -ik...?; *to get the train*
  yaakhud il-aTr

get back: we get back
  tomorrow (verb) **nirgaA**
  bokra
get in (verb) **yudkhul;**
  (arrive) **yowSal**
get off (verb) (bus, etc) **yinzil**
get out (verb) **yukhrug**
get up (verb) (rise)
  yi'oom
gift **hideyya**
girl **bint**
girls **banaat**
give (verb) **yeddee,**
  yeAtee
glad (adj) **mabsooT;** *I'm*
  glad **ana mabsooT**
glass (material) **izaaz,**
  zugaag; (for drinking)
  kubayya
glasses (eye)
  naDaara
gloves **gwantee**
glue **samgh**
go/going (verb) **raayiH:**
  raayiH/raayHa/raayHeen
  (m/f/pl)
goggles **naDaarit**
  mayya
gold **dahab**
good (adj) **kwayyis;**
  good morning
  sabaaH il-kheir; *good*
  afternoon/evening
  masaa' il-kheir
goodbye **maA as-salaama**
government **Hukooma**
granddaughter **Hafeeda**
grandfather **gidd**
grandmother **gidda**
grandson **Hafeed**
grapes **ainab**
grass (lawn) **Hasheesh,**
  Aushb
Great Britain **bireeTaanya**
  il-Auzma
great! (adj) **Aazeem!**
Greece **il-yoonaan**
Greek (adj) **yoonaanee**
green (adj) (m/f) **akhDar/**
  khaDra
gray (adj) **ramaadee**
grill **shawwaaya**
grilled (adj) **mashwee**
grocer **ba'aal**
ground floor **id-door**
  il-arDee
guarantee (noun) **Damaan;**
  (verb) **yiDman**
guard **Haaris**
guest **Deif**

guidebook (travel guide)
  daleel siyaaHi
guitar **gitaar**
Gulf **il-khaleeg;** *Gulf States*
  duwwal il-khaleeg
gun (rifle) **bundu'eeya;**
  (pistol) **musaddas**

H

hair **shaAr**
hair dryer **sishwaar**
haircut (for man) **Helaaqit**
  ish-shaAr; (for woman)
  ass ish-shaAr
hairdresser **Hallaaq,**
  kwaafeer
half **nus;** *half an hour* **nus**
  saaAa *half past two*
  itnein wi-nus
hammer **shakoosh, miTraqa**
hand **yad, eed**
hand sanitizer **muAaqqem**
  edeen
handbag **shanTat yad**
hand brake **faraamil yad**
handkerchief **mandeel**
handle (door) **mi'baD**
handsome (adj) **waseem**
happy (adj) **saAeed,**
  mabsooT
harbor **meena**
hard (adj) (tough) **naashif,**
  qaasee; (difficult)
  saAb
hat **burneita, qubaAa**
have (verb) **Aand: Aandee/**
  Aandina (m/f/pl); *I have...*
  Aandee...; *I don't have...*
  ma Aandeesh...; *have you*
  got ...? **Andak/-ik...?;** *can I*
  have...? **mumkin...?;** *I have*
  to go now **laazim**
  amshee dilwa'tee; (own)
  yamtalik
hay fever **Homma l-'ash**
he **howwa**
head **raas**
head office **markaz**
  ra'eesee
headache **sodaaA**
headlights **fanoos**
  (amaamee)
headphones **sammaAaat**
  raas
hear (verb) **yismaA**
hearing aid **sammaAaat**
  il-asamm
hearing loop **al Halaqa**
  AssamAia

heart **alb**; (cards) **oloob**
heart attack **nawba albeyya**
heating **tadfe'a**
heavy (adj) **ti'eel**
heel **kaAb**
hello **ahlan**; (when answering telephone) **aaloh**
help (noun) **musaaAada**; (verb) **yisaaAid**; help! **in-nagda!**; can I help you? **ayyi khidma?**
hepatitis **iltihaab kabidi**
her: it's her **dee heyya**; it's for her **dah Aalashaan-ha**; (possessive) **...-ha**; her book **ketaabha**;
her (contd.) her house **beitha**; it's hers **dah bitaaAha**
here **hina**
hi **salaam**
hieroglyphs **heeroghleefee**
high (adj) **Aaalee**
highway code **taAleemaat il-qiyaada**
hill **tell**
him: it's him **dah howwa**; it's for him **dah Aalashaan-uh**
hire (verb) **yia'ggar, yista'gir**
his **...-uh**; his book **ketaabuh**; his house **beituh**; it's his **dah bitaaAuh**
history **taareekh**
hitchhiking **safar magganee/taTaffulee**
HIV positive (adj) **mareeD 'eidz**
hobby **hiwaaya**
holiday **agaaza, AuTla**
Holland **holanda**
honest (adj) **saadi', ameen**
honey **Aasal**
honeymoon **shahr il-Aasal**
hood (car) **kabboot**
horn (car) **kalaks**; (animal) **arn**
horrible (adj) **fazeeA**
horse **Husaan**
horse riding **rokoob il-kheil**
hose **kharToom**
hospital **mustashfa**
host **saaHib il-beit**
hostess **saHbit il-beit**

hot (adj) (water) (mayya) **sukhn**; (weather) **Harr**
hotel **fundu'**
hour **saaAa**
house **beit, manzil**
household products **muntagaat manzileyya**
how? **izzay?**; how many? **kaam?**; how much? **bikaam?**
hundred **meyya**
hungry: I'm hungry (adj) **ana gAaaan**
hurry: I'm in a hurry (adj) **ana mustaAgil**
husband **zoog**

I

I **ana**
ice **talg**
ice cream **ays kreem**
ice cube **Hittit talg**
ice pop **maSSaasit ays kreem**
identification **ithbaat shakhSeyya**
if **iza, lau**
ignition **ik-kontakt**
ill (adj) **mareeD**
immediately **fawran**
important (adj) **muHimm**
impossible (adj) **mustaHeel**
in **fi**; in English **bil ingleezee**; in the hotel **fil-fundu'**
included (adj) **shaamil**
India **il-hind**
Indian (man) **hindee**; (woman) **hindeyya**; (adj) **hindee**
indigestion **Ausr haDm**
infection **Adwa, iltihaab**
information **maAloomaat**
inhaler (for asthma, etc) **bakh-khaakha**
injection **Hu'na**
injury **isaaba**
ink **Hibr**
inner tube **anboob daakhilee**
insect **Hashara**
insect repellent **Taarid lil-Hasharaat**
inside **daakhil**
insomnia **araq**
insurance **ta'meen**

interest (hobby) **hiwaaya**
interesting (adj) **shayyiq**
internet **internet**
interpret (verb) **yitargim fawry**
intersection **taqaatuA**
invitation **Aozooma, daAwa**
invite (verb) **yiAzim**
invoice **fatoora**
Iraq **il-Airaaq**
Ireland **ayirlanda**
Irish (adj) **ayirlandee**
Irishman **ayirlandee**
Irishwoman **ayirlandeyya**
iron (metal) **Hadeed**; (for clothes) **makwa**
ironmonger **Haddaad**
is: he is... **howwa...**; she is... **heyya...**
Islam **islaam**
island **gazeera**
it **howwa, heyya**; it's over there **howwa/heyya hinaak**
Italy **eeTaalya**
itch (noun) **Hakka gildeeya, harsh**

J

jacket **jaketta**
jam **murabba**
January **yanaayir**
jazz **mooseeqa il-jazz**
jealous (adj) **ghayraan**
jeans **jeenz**
jellyfish **qandeel il-baHr**
jeweler **gawaahirgee**
job **wazeefa**
joke **nukta**
Jordan **il-urdunn**
journal **mufakkera**
journey **riHla**
juice **Aaseer**
juice bar **maHal Aaseer**
July **yoolyo**
June **yoonyo**
just: he's just gone out **lissa khaarig**; just two **itnein bass**

K

key **moftaaH**
keyboard **keeboord**
kidney **kilya**
kilo **keelo**
kilometer **keelometr**
kitchen **maTbakh**

knee **rukba**
knife **sikkeen**
knitting **it-tereeko**
know (verb) **yaAraf**;
   I don't know **ma
   aArafsh**
Kuwait **il-kuweit**

L

label **bitaa'a**
lace **dantella**
laces (of shoe) **robaaт
   il-gazma**
lake **buнeira**
lamb **kharoof soghayyar**
lamp **lamba, misbaaн**
lampshade **abajoora**
land (noun) **arD**; (verb)
   yuhbuт
language **lugha**
lantern **fanoos**
laptop **laabtob**
large (adj) **kibeer**
last (adj) (final) **akheer**;
   last week **il-usbooA illi
   faat**; last month **ish
   shahr illi faat**; at last!
   akheeran!
late (adj) **mit'akh-khar**;
   the bus is late **il-otobees
   mit'akh khar**
later **baAdein**
laugh (verb) **yiDнak**
laundromat **maghsala**
laundry (place) **maghsala**;
   (dirty clothes) **il-ghaseel**;
   (soap) **masнoo' ghaseel**
law **qanoon**; (subject of
   study) **il-нuqooq**
lawn mower **makanit ass
   il-нasheesh**
lawyer **muhaamee**
laxative **mussah-hil**
lazy (adj) **kaslaan**
lead (dog) **нabl**
leaf **wara'it shagar**
learn (verb) **yitAallim**
leather **gild**
leave (verb) **yiseeb**
Lebanon **libnaan**
lecture **muнaдra**
lecture hall **qaaAit
   muнaдraat**
lecturer (university)
   muнaaдer gaamAee
left (not right) **shimaal,
   yasaar**
left luggage (locker)
   khizaanit shonaт

leg **rigl**
leisure time **wa't
   il-faraagh**
lemon **lamoon**
lemonade **lamoonaata**
length **тool**
lens **Aadasa**
less **a'all**
lesson **dars**
letter (mail) **gawaab**;
   (alphabet) **нarf**
lettuce **khass**
library **maktaba**
Libya **leebya**
license plate **looнit
   il-arqaam**
life **нayaa**
life jacket **sutrit
   in-najaah**
lift (in building) **asanseir,
   misAad**; could you give
   me a lift? **mumkin
   tiwassalnee?**
light (adj) (not heavy)
   khafeef; (not dark)
   faatiн; (illumination)
   noor
lighter **wallaaAa**
like (verb) **biyнibb: baнib/
   binнib** (m/f/pl); I like
   swimming **ana baнib
   is-sibaaнa**; that's
   like... **dah zayy...**; what
   does he look like? **shakloo
   eh?**
lime (fruit) **lamoon**
line **khaтт**; the line is busy
   il-khaтт mashghool
lip balm **marham
   shafaayif**
lipstick **rooj**
list **qaa'ima, lista**
literature **adab**
liter **litr**
little (adj) (small) **sughayyar**;
   just a little **shwayya
   bass**
liver (human) **kabid**
living room **ghurfit guloos**
lobster **estakooza**
local (adj) **maнallee**
lollipop **massaasa**
long (adj) **тaweel**; how long
   does it take? **yaakhud
   ad eh?**
lorry **looree**
lost: I'm lost! (adj) **ana tuht!**
lost property **mafqoodaat**
lot: a lot **kiteer,
   kimeeya kibeera**

loud (adj) (noise) **Aaalee**;
   (color) **sarikh**
lounge **saala**
love (noun) **нubb**;
   (verb) **yiнibb**
lover (man) **Asheeq**;
   (woman) **Asheeqa**
low (adj) **waaтi, munkhafiD**
luck **нazz**; good luck!
   нazz saAeed!
luggage **shonaт, нaqaa'eb**
luggage rack **raff
   il-нaqaa'eb**
lunch **ghada**

M

magazine **magalla**
mail **bareed**
mail box **sundoo'
   il-bareed**
main street **shaareA
   ra'eesee**
make (verb) (manufacture)
   yasnaA
make-up **makyaaj**
man **raagil**
manager **mudeer**
map **khareeтa**; a map of
   Riyadh **khareeтit
   ir-riyaaD**; online maps
   kharayet al-internet
marble **rukhaam**
March **maaris**
margarine **samn
   nabaatee**
market **soo'**
marmalade **murabbit
   burtu'aan**
married (adj) **mitgawwiz**
mascara **maskaara**
mass (church) **quddaas**
mast **saaree**
match (light) **kabreet**;
   (sports) **maтsh, mubaara**
material (cloth) **umaash**
matter: what's the matter?
   maalak?
mattress **martaba**
Mauritania **moretaanya**
May **maayo**
maybe **yimkin**
me: it's me (speaking) **ana
   batkallim**; it's for me
   dah Aalashaanee
meal **wagba**
meat **laнma, laнm**
mechanic **mikaneekee**
medicine **dawa**; (subject
   of study) **iт-тibb**

meet (verb) **yi'aabil**
meeting **igtimaaA**
melon **shammaam**
men's restroom **twaalett lir-rigaal**
menu **menu, qaa'ima**
message **risaala**
microwave **mikroweiv**
midday **iD-Duhr**
middle: in the middle **fil-wesT**
midnight **nus il-leil**
milk **Haleeb, laban**
mine: it's mine **dah bitaaAee**
mineral water **mayya maAdaneyya**
mint **naAnaaA**
minute **da'ee'a;** *five minutes* **khamas da'aayi'**
mirror **miraaya**
Miss **aanisa**
mistake **ghalTa;** (verb) *to make a mistake* **yighlaT**
mobile (phone) **mubayil, maHmool, gawwaal**
modem **modem**
monastery **deir**
Monday **(yoom) il-itnein**
money **fuloos**
monitor (computer) **shaasha**
month **shahr**
monument **nusub tizkaaree**
moon **amar**
more **aktar**
morning **SabaaH;** *in the morning* **is-SubH, fis SabaaH**
Morocco **il-maghrib**
mosaic **fosayfesaa'**
mosque **masgid, gaamiA**
mosquito **naamoosa, baAooDa**
mother **umm, waalida**
mother-in-law **Hamat**
mother-of-pearl **sadaf**
motorcycle **motosikl**
motorboat **lansh, qaareb**
motorway **Tareeq Horr**
mountain **gabal**
mouse **faar**
mustache **shanab**
mouth **bo'**
move (verb) **yitHarrak;** *don't move!* **ma titHarraksh;** (verb) (move house) **yiAzzil**

movie **film**
movies **is-seenima**
Mr. **il-ustaaz, is-sayyid**
Mrs. **il-ustaaza, is-sayyida**
much: not much **mish kiteer;** *much better* **aHsan kiteer**
mug **fingaan kibeer**
mule **baghl**
mom **maama**
museum **matHaf**
mushroom **fiTr**
music **mooseeqa**
musical instrument **aalaa mooseeqeyya**
musician **mooseeqaar**
Muslim **muslim**
mussels **umm il-khulool**
mustard **mostarDa, khardal**
my **...-ee;** *my book* **kitaabee;** *my bag* **shanTitee;** *my keys* **mafaateeHee**
mythology **asaaTeer**

N

nail (metal) **mosmaar**
nails (finger) **Dawaafir**
nail file **mabrad Dawaafir**
name **ism**
napkin **foo-Ta**
narrow (adj) **Dayya'**
near (adj) **urrayyib min, ganb**
necessary (adj) **Darooree**
neck **ra'aba**
necklace **Au'd**
need (verb) **yiHtaag;** *I need...* **ana miHtaag ...;** *there's no need* **mafeesh daaAee**
needle **ibra**
negative (adj) **salbee**
nephew (brother's son) **ibn il-akh;** (sister's son) **ibn il-ukht**
never **abadan**
nevermind **maAlesh**
new (adj) **gideed**
New Zealand **niyoo zilanda**
New Zealander (man) **niyoo zilandee;** (woman) **niyoo zilandeyya;** (adj, depending on position in a sentence) **niyoo zilandee**
news **akhbaar**

news agent **maHal is-suHuf**
newspaper **gornaal, gareeda**
next **ig-gaay;** *next week* **il-usbooA ig-gaay;** *next month* **ish-shahr ig-gaay**
next to **ganb**
nice (adj) **kwayyis, gameel**
niece (brother's daughter) **bint il-akh;** (sister's daughter) **bint il-ukht**
night **leila;** *three nights* **talat leyaalee**
night doorman **mudeer laylee**
nightclub **malha laylee, nayt clab**
nightdress **amees noom**
Nile **in-neel**
nine **tisAa**
no (response) **laa;** *I have no...* **maa Andeesh...;** *there are no...* **ma feesh...**
noisy (adj) **dawsha**
north **shamaal**
Northern Ireland **ayirlanda ish-shamaaleyya**
nose **anf**
not **mish**
notepad **nota**
nothing **walla Haaga**
novel **riwaaya**
November **novamber**
now **dilwa'ti**
number **raqm, nimra**
nurse **mumarriD**
nut (for bolt) **saamoola**
nuts (dried fruit) **mikassaraat**

O

o'clock: 3 o'clock **is-saAa talaata**
obelisk **masalla**
occasionally **aHyaanan**
October **octoobar**
octopus **akhTaboot**
of course **taHt Amrukum**
office **maktab**
often **kiteer, ghaaliban**
oil (for food, engine) **zeit;** (crude) **betrool**
oil industry **sinaaAit il-betrool**
oil wells **aabaar betrool**
ointment **marham**
OK **maashi, Tayyib, kwayyis**
old (adj) (thing) **adeem;** (person) **Aagooz**

olives **zaytoon**
Oman **Aomaan**
omelet **omlet**
on **Aala**; on the ground
   Aalal-arD
one **waaHid**
onion **basal**
only **bass, faqaT**
open (verb) **yiftaH**;
   (adj) **maftooH**
opening hours **mawaAeed**
   il-Aamal
opera **obra**
opera house **daar**
   il-obra
operating room **ghurfit**
   il-Aamaliyyat
opposite: opposite the hotel
   udaam il-fundu'
optician **mutakhasses**
   naDaaraat
or **aw**
orange (adj) (colour)
   borto'aanee; (fruit)
   borto'aan
orange juice **Aaseer**
   borto'aan
orchestra **orkestra**
ordinary (adj) (normal)
   Aadee
organ **AuDw**; (music)
   org
our **-na**; it's ours **dah**
   bitaaAna
out: he's out **howwa mish**
   mawgood
out of order **Aatlaan**
outside **barra, khaarig**
oven **furn**
over **foo'**; over there
   hinaak
overtake (verb) **yit-khaTTa**

P

package **Tard**
packet **Ailba**; a packet of...
   Ailbit...
padlock **ifl**
page **safHa**
pain **alam**
paint (noun) **booya**
pair **gooz**
pajamas **bijaama**
Pakistan **baakistaan**
Pakistani (man)
   baakistaanee; (woman)
   baakistaaneyya; (adj)
   baakistaanee
Palestine **filasTeen**

Palestinian (man)
   filasTeenee; (woman)
   filasTeeneyya; (adj)
   filasTeenee
palm **nakhla**
pants **banTaloon**
paper (material) **waraq**
papyrus **waraq bardee**
parcel **Tard**
pardon? **naAam? afandim?**
parents **waalidein**
park (noun) **gineina,**
   Hadeeqa; (verb) **arkin**;
   where can I park? **arkin**
   fein?
party (celebration) **Hafla**;
   (group) **magmooAa**;
   (political) **Hizb**
passenger **raakib**
passport **gawaaz is-safar**
passport control **noqtat**
   al-gawazaat
password **kilmit il-muroor**
pasta **makarona**
path **mamarr, mamsha**
pay (verb) **yidfaA**
payment **dafA**
peach **khookh**
peanuts **fool soodaanee**
pear **kommetra**
pearl **lu'lu'**
peas **bisilla**
pedestrian **mushaa**
peg (clothes) **mashbak**
   ghaseel
pen **alam**
pencil **alam rusaas**
pencil sharpener **barraaya**
penpal **sadeeq bil**
   muraasla
penicillin **binsileen**
peninsula **shibh gazeera**
people **naas**
pepper **filfil**
peppermints **niAnaaA**
per: per night **fil leila**
perfect (adj) **kaamil**
perfume **AiTr**
pergola **bergoola**
perhaps **yimkin, rubbama**
perm **tamweeg ish-shaAr**
person **shakhs**;
   per person **in-nafar**
Pharaoh **farAoon**
pharmacy **saydaleyya**
photograph (noun) **soora**;
   (verb) **yisawwar**
photographer **musawwir**
phrase book **kitaab**
   TaAbeeraat

piano **biyaano**
pickpocket **nash-shaal**
picnic **nuzha**
piece **Hitta, qiTaa**
pillow **makhadda**
pilot (of aircraft) **Tayyaar**
pin **dabboos**
PIN (ATM) **erraqam esseree**
pine (tree) **shagarit**
   sonoobar
pineapple **ananaas**
pink (adj) **wardee, bamba**
pipe (smoking) **beeba**
   (construction, etc)
   maasoora, anbooba
pistons **basaatim**
pitcher **abreeq**
pizza **beetza**
place **makaan**
plant **zarA, nabaat**
plaster (for cut) **blaaster**
plastic **blaastik**
plastic bag **kees blaastik**
plate **Taba'**
platform **raseef**
play (theatre) **masraHeyya**
please **min faDlak**
plug (electrical) **kobs**;
   (sink) **saddaada**
plumber **sabbaak**
pocket **geib**
police **shurTee**
police officer **zaabiT**
police report **maHDar**
police station **markaz ish-**
   shurTa
politics **siyyaasa**
pond **birka**
poor (adj) **fa'eer**; (bad
   quality) **radee'**
pop music **mooseeqa**
   gharbee
pork **laHm khanzeer**
port (harbor) **meena**
porter (for luggage)
   shayyaal
possible **mumkin**
post (noun) **bareed**;
   (verb) **yursil bil-bareed**
post box **sundoo' bareed**
post office **maktab**
   il-bareed
postcard **bitaa'a**
   bareedyya
postman **saaAee il-bareed**
potato **baTaaTis**
poultry **id-dawaagin**
pound (money) **gineih**;
   (weight) **raTl**
powder **bodra**

prawn **gambaree**
prayer mat **siggaadit salaa**
prefer (verb) **yifaDDal**
prescription **roshetta**
pretty (adj) (beautiful)
  gameel
price **siAr**
priest **issees**
printer **makaniT TebaaAa**
private (adj) **khaass**
problem **mushkila**; what's
  the problem? **eh
  il-mushkila**; no problem
  mafeesh mushkila
professor **ustaaz**
profits **arbaaH**
proposal (business) **AarD**
public (adj) (general) **Aaam**
public holiday **agaaza
  rasmeyya**
pull (verb) **yisHab**
puncture (tyre) **Aagala
  nayma**
purple (adj) **banafsigee**
purse **maHfaza, kees**
push (verb) **yizo',
  yidfaA**
pyramids **il-ahraam(aat)**

Q

Qatar **qaTar**
quality **gawda**
quay **raseef il-meena**
question **soo'aal**
queue (noun) **saff**;
  (verb) **yo'af fis saff**
quick (adj) **sareeA**
quiet (adj) **haadee**
Quran **il-qur'aan**

R

rabbit **arnab**
radiator **radyateer**
radio **radyo**
radish **figl**
railroad **issikkal-Hadeed**
rain **maTar**
raincoat **balTo maTar**
raisins **zibeeb**
rake **shooka**
rare (adj) (uncommon)
  naadir; (steak) **sewaa
  aleel**
rat **faar**
razor blades **emwaas**
read (verb) **yi'ra**
ready (adj) **gaahiz,
  mustaAidd**

ready meals **wagbaat
  gahza**
rear lights **fanoos khalfee**
receipt **wasl**
reception **Haflat isti'baal**
record (music) **usTuwaana**;
  (sporting etc) **raqam**
  qiyaasee
red (adj) (m/f) **aHmar/
  Hamra**
Red Sea **il-baHr il-aHmar**
refreshments **muraTTibaat**
registered post **bareed
  musaggal**
relatives **araayib**
relax (verb) **yistirayyaH**
religion **deen, deeyaana**
remember (verb) **yiftikir**;
  I don't remember **mish
  faakir**
rent (verb) **yi'aggar**;
  (noun) **eegaar**
repair (verb) **yisallaH**;
  (noun) **tasleeH**
report (noun) **taqreer**
research **abHaath**
reservation **Hagz**
reserve (verb) **yiHgiz**
rest (remainder) **il-baa'ee**;
  (verb) (relax) **istiraaHa**
restaurant **maTAam**
return (verb) (come back)
  yirgaA; (give back)
  yiraggaA
return (ticket) **dhahaab
  w-Aawda**
rice **ruz**
rich (adj) (wealthy person);
  ghanee (heavy food)
  te'eel
right (adj) (correct) **saHeeH**;
  (direction) **yimeen**;
  (right away) **Haalan**
ring (verb) (to call) **yitassil
  bit-tilifoon**; (wedding,
  etc) **khaatim, dibla**
ripe (adj) **mistewi**
river **nahr**
robbery **sir'a**
robe **galabeyya**
road **Tareeq, shaareA**
roasted (adj) **fil-furn**
rock (stone) **sakhr**
roll (bread) **Aeish,
  khubz**
roof **satH**
room **ghurfa**; (space)
  makaan
room service **khidmit
  il-ghuraf**

rope **Habl**
roses **ward**
round (adj) (circular)
  daa'iree
row boat **markib tagdeef**
rubber (material) **kawetsh**
ruby (gemstone)
  yaaqoot aHmar
rucksack **shanTat Dahr**
rug (mat) **siggaada**;
  (blanket) **baTaneyya**
ruins **aTlaal, anqaaD**
ruler (for drawing) **masTara**
run (verb) **yigree**
running **garey**

S

sad (adj) **Hazeen**
safe (adj) **fi amaan**
safety pin **dabboos amaan**
sailing **il-ibHaar**
sail boat/felucca **markib
  shiraaAee**
salad **salaTa**
sale (at reduced prices)
  okazyoon
sales (company)
  mabeeAaat
salmon **salamon**
salt **malH**
same: the same dress **nafs
  il-fustaan**; the same
  people **nafs il-ashkhaas**;
  same again **kamaan
  waaHid**
sand **raml**
sand dunes **kuthbaan**
sandals **sandal**
sandwich **sandawitsh**
sanitary napkins **fowaT
  seHHeyya**
Saturday **(yoom) is-sabt**
sauce **salsa**
saucepan **Halla**
Saudi Arabia
  is-saAoodeeya
sauna **sawna**
sausage **sugu'**
say (verb) **yi'ool**; what did
  you say? **ult eh?**; how do
  you say ...? **izzay ti'ool ...?**
scarf **kofeyya**; (Islamic
  headscarf) **Higaab**
schedule **gadwal**
school **madrasa**
science (subject of study)
  il-Auloom
scissors **ma'ass**
scorpion **Aqrab**

Scotland **iskotlanda**
Scottish (adj) **iskotlandee**
screen (computer) **shaasha**
screw **mismaar alawooz**
screwdriver **mafak**
sea **baHr**
seafood **makoolaat il-baHr**
seat **kursee, maqAad**
seat belt **Hizaam il-maqaAd**
second (of time) **sanya;**
    (in series) **it-taanee**
secretary **sekerteir/a**
see (verb) **yishoof;** I can't
    see **ana mish shayyif;**
    I see (verb) (understand)
    fihimt
self-employed **Aamel Hor**
sell (verb) **yibeeA**
seminar **Halaqa diraasyya**
send (verb) **yibAat**
separate (adj) **munfasil;**
    (verb) **yifsil**
separated (adj) (man)
    munfasil; (woman)
    munfasila
September **septamber**
serious (adj) **khaTeer**
server (waiter) **garson**
service **khidma**
serviette **fooTa lil-maa'ida**
seven **sabAa**
sew (verb) **yikhayyaT**
shampoo **shamboo**
shave (noun) **Hilaa'a;**
    (verb) **yiHla'**
shaving cream **raghwit**
    Hilaa'a
shawl **shaal**
she **heyya**
sheep **kharoof**
sheet **milaaya**
shells (sea) **sadaf**
ship **safeena**
shirt **amees**
shoe polish **warneesh**
    il-gazma
shoe store **maHal gizam**
shoelaces **robaaT il-gazma**
shoes **gazma, gizam**
shop **maHal**
shopkeeper **saaheb maHal**
shopping **tasawwuq;**
    (verb) to go shopping
    yitsawwaq
short (adj) **'usayyar**
shorts **short**
shoulder **kitf**
shower (bath) **dush;** (rain)
    maTar
shower gel **jil istiHmaam**

shrimp **gambaree**
shutter (camera) **Haagib**
    il-Adasa; (window)
    sheesh
siblings **ikhwaat**
sick (adj) (ill) **mareeD**
side (edge) **Harf**
sidelights **anwaar**
    gaanebeyya
sidewalk **raseef**
sights **maAaalim, manaazir**
sightseeing **ziyaarit**
    il-maAaalim
sign **looHa;** (verb) **yimDee,**
    yiwaqqaA; (noun)
    yafTa
silk **Hareer**
silver (adj) (color) **faDDee;**
    (metal) **faDDa**
SIM card **sim-kart**
simple (adj) **baseeT**
sing (verb) **yighannee**
single (one) **waaHid;**
    (adj) (unmarried) **Aazib**
single room **ghurfa**
    li-shakhs
sink (noun) **HooD**
sister **ukht**
sitting room **ghurfit guloos**
six **sitta**
size **ma'aas**
skin cleanser **munazzif**
    lil-bashra
skirt **jeeba, tannoora**
sky **samaa**
skyscraper **naaTiHat**
    saHaab
sleep (noun) **noom;** (verb)
    yinaam; to go to
    sleep **yinaam**
sleeping pill **Huboob**
    munawwima
sleeve **komm**
slippers **shibshib**
slow (adj) **baTee'**
small (adj) **sughayyar**
small boat **'aareb**
smell (noun) **reeHa;** (verb:
    transitive) **yishimm**
smile (noun) **ibtisaama;**
    (verb) **yibtisim**
smoke (noun) **dukhaan;**
    (verb) **yidakh-khan**
smoking **tadkheen;**
    non-smoking **doon**
    tadkheen
snack **wagba khafeefa**
snorkeling **snurkeling;**
    snorkeling gear **Aiddit**
    snurkeling

snow **galeed**
so: so good! **kwayyis**
    giddan!
soap **saboon**
soccer **koorat il-qadam**
socks **sharabaat**
soda water **sooda**
sofa **kanaba**
soft (adj) **Tari**
Somalia **is-somaal**
somebody **Hadd**
something **Haaga**
sometimes **aHyaanan,**
    saaAaat
son **ibn**
song **ughniya**
sorry! **aasif!;** I'm sorry **ana**
    aasif
soup **shorba**
south **ganoob**
South Africa **ganoob ifriqya**
South African (man)
    ganoob ifriqee;
    (woman) **ganoob**
    ifriqeyya; (adj) **ganoob**
    ifriqee
souvenir **tizkaar**
spade (shovel) **garoof;**
    (cards) **il-bastohnee**
spare parts **qiTaA ghiyaar**
spark plugs **boojeehaat**
speak (verb) (oneself)
    yitkallim; speak to
    (someone else) **yikallim;**
    do you speak...?
    bititkallim(ee)...?; I don't
    speak... **maa**
    batkallimsh...
speed **surAa**
speed limit **Hadd is-surAa**
speedometer **Aaddaad**
    is-surAa
Sphinx **abul-hool**
spice shop **Attar**
spider **Ankaboot**
spinach **sabaanikh**
spoon **maAla'ah**
sports **riyaaDa**
sports field **naadee**
    riyaaDee
spring (mechanical) **sosta;**
    (season) **ir-rabeeA**
sprinkler **rash-shaash**
square (town) **midaan**
stadium **istaad**
stairs **salaalim**
stamp **TaabiA bareed;**
    stamps **TawaabiA**
    bareed
stapler **dabbaasa**

star **nigma**
start (verb: intransitive)
   yibtidee
starters **muqabbelaat**
statement **efaada**
station **maнaттa**
statue **timsaal**
steak **bofteik**
steal (verb) **yisra'**; it's been
   stolen **etsara'**
steering wheel **Agalit
   il-qiyaada, diriksiyoon**
stewardess **muдeefa**
sting (noun) **ladgha**;
   (verb) **yildagh**
stockings **sharabaat
   нareemee**
stomach **baтn, maаida**
stomachache **maghas**
stop (verb) (transitive)
   yuwa'af; (intransitive)
   yu'af; (bus stop)**maнaттit
   otobees**; stop! **qif!**
storm **Aaasifa**
stove **butagaaz**
straight on **Aala тool**
strawberry **faraawla**
street **shaareA**
string (cord) **doobaara**;
   (guitar etc) **watar**
stroller **Arabeyyiт aтfaal**
student **тaalib**
stupid (adj) **ghabee**
suburbs **дawaaнee**
Sudan **is-soodaan**
sugar **sukkar**
suit (noun) **badla**; (verb)
   yinaasib; that suits me
   dah yinaasibnee
suitcase **shanтa**
sun **shams**
sun cream **kereem
   ish-shams**
sunbath **нammaam shams**
sunburn **нar'it shams**
Sunday **(yoom) il-нad**
sunglasses **naдaarit shams**
sunny (adj) **moshmis**
sunstroke **дarbit shams**
suntan **samaar**
supermarket **supermarkit**
supplement **guz' iдaafee**
suppository **loboos**
sure (adj) **akeed**
surname **ism il Aeila**
sweat (noun) **Araq**;
   (verb) **yiАra'**
sweater **buloovar**
sweet (adj) (not sour) **нelew**
swelling **waram**

swim (verb) **yisbaн**
swim suit **mayoh**
swimmer **sabbaaн**
swimming **is-sibaaнa**
swimming pool
   нammaam sibaaнa
swimming trunks **mayoh**
switch (light, etc)
   moftaaн
Switzerland **sweesra**
synagogue **maаbad
   il-yahood**
Syria **suriya**
syrup (medicinal)
   dawa shorb

T

table **tarabeeza**
tablets **нuboob**
take/taking (verb) **waakhid:
   haakhud/hanakhud**
   (m/f/pl)
talcum powder **boodrit
   talk**
talk (verb) **yitkallim**
tall (adj) **тaweel**
tap **нanafeyya**
taxi **taaksi**
taxi stand **mawqaf taaksi**
tea **shaay**
teacher **mudarris**
telephone (noun) **tilifoon**;
   (verb) **yitassil bit
   tilifoon** telephone call
   mukalma tilifooneyya
telephone number
   nimrit it-tilifoon
television **tilifizyoon**
ten **Aashra**
tennis **tinis**
tent **kheima**
tent peg **wattad
   il-kheima**
tent pole **Aamood nasb
   il-kheima**
terminal (airport, etc)
   saala
tests (medical) **taнaaleel**
thank (verb) **yushkur**; thank
   you/thanks **shukran**;
   thank you very much
   shukran gazeelan
that: that cup **il-fingaan
   dah**; that man **il-raagil
   dah**; that woman **is-sitt
   dee**; what's that? **eh
   dah?**; I think that...
   aАtaqid an...
theater **masraн**

their **...-hum**; their room
   ghurfithum; their books
   kutubhum; it's theirs
   dah bitaaАhum
them: it's for them **dah
   Aalashaan-hum**
there **hinaak**; there is/are...
   feeh...; there isn't/aren't...
   ma feesh...
thermos **tormos**
these: these things
   il-нaagaat dool; these
   men **ir-riggaala dool**;
   these are mine
   dool bitooАee
they **humma**
thick (adj) **sameek**
thief **нaraamee**
thin (adj) **rufayyaА**
think: I think so (verb)
   aАtaqid; I'll think about it
   нafakkar fil-mawдooА
third (adj) **it-taalit**
thirsty: I'm thirsty (adj)
   ana aтshaan
this **dah/dee**; this cup
   il-fingaan dah; this man
   il-raagil dah; this woman
   is-sitt dee; what's this?
   eh dah?
those: those things
   il-нaagaat dool; those
   men **ir-riggaala dool**;
   those are mine
   dool bitooАee
thousand **alf**
three **talaata**
throat **zoor**
throat lozenge **baasteeliya
   liz-zoor**
through **khilaal**
thunderstorm **Aasifa
   raАdeeya**
Thursday **(yoom)
   il-khamees**
ticket **tazkara**
ticket office **shibbaak
   tazaakir**
tie (noun) **kravatta**;
   (verb) **yurbuт**
tights **sharaab тaweel**
tiles **issirameek**
time **wa't, saaАa**; what
   time is it? **issaaАa kaam?**
timetable **gadwal
   mawaАeed**
tip (money) **ba'sheesh**;
   (end) **тarf**
tired (adj) **taАbaan**; I feel
   tired **ashАur bi-taАb**

tissues **manadeel wara'**
to **li**; *quarter to two*
   itnein illa rubа
toast **tost**
tobacco **dukh-khaan**
today **innahaarda,**
   il-yoom
together **maаa baаd**
toilet paper **wara' twaalett**
toilets **twaalett,**
   нammaamaat
tomato **тamaаtim**
tomato juice **аaseer**
   тamaаtim
tomorrow **bokra**
tongue **lisaan**
tonight **il-leila** (dee)
too (also) **kamaan;**
   (excessive) **giddan,**
   awee
tooth **sinn**
toothache **alam asnaan**
toothbrush **furshit asnaan**
toothpaste **maаgoon**
   asnaan
tour **gawla**
tour guide **murshid**
   syaнee
tourist **saаyeн**
tourist office **maktab**
   siyaана
towel **fooтa**
tower **borg**
town **madeena, balad**
toy **liаba**
toy shop **maнal liаab**
tractor **garraar**
trade fair **maаrad**
   tugaaree
traditions **taqaaleed**
traffic **muroor**
traffic jam **azmit muroor**
traffic lights **ishaaraat**
   elmuroor
trailer **maqтoora**
train **'атr**
train station **maнaттit**
   il'атr
trainee **taнt it-tamreen**
translate (verb) **yitargim**
trash **zibaala**
trash can **safeehit**
   zibaala
travel agency **wikaalit**
   safareeyaat
tray **ѕeneyya**
tree **shagara;** *trees* **shagar**
trip **riнla**
trousers **banтaloon**
trunk (car) **shanтa**

try (verb) (test) **yigarrab;**
   (make an effort)
   yiнaawil
Tuesday **(yoom) ittalaat**
Tunisia **toonis**
tunnel **nafa'**
Turkey **turkeya**
turn: turn left/right (verb)
   khud shimaal/yimeen
tweezers **mil'aат**
twin room **ghurfa**
   muzdawaga
two **itnein**
tire **kawitsh, iтaar**

U

ugly (adj) **wehesh**
umbrella **shamseyya**
uncle (paternal) **аmm;**
   (maternal) **khaal**
under **taнt**
underground **taнt il-ard**
underpants (men) **kalsoon**
understand (verb) **yifham;**
   I don't understand **mish**
   faahim
underwear **malaabis**
   daakhileyya
university **gamаa**
unmarried (adj) **аaazib**
until **leнadd, leghaayit**
unusual (adj) **gheir аadee**
up **foo'**
urgent (adj) **mistaаgil**
urn **zeer**
us: it's for us **dah**
   аalashaan-na
use (noun) **fayda;** (verb)
   yistakhdim, yistaаmil
useful (adj) **mufeed**
useless (adj) **gheir mufeed**
usual (adj) **аadee**
usually **аadatan**

V

vacant (adj) (rooms)
   (ghuraf) faдya
vaccination **liqaaн**
vacuum cleaner **maknasa**
   kahrabaa'eyya
valley **waadee**
valve **simaam**
vanilla **vanelia**
vase **vaaza**
veal **bitello**
vegetables **khuдaar**
vegetarian **nabaatee**
vehicle **аarabyya**

very **giddan, awee**
vest **amees тaнtaanee**
vet **doktoor beтaree**
video games **alаaab**
   il-vidyoo
video tape **shireet vidyo**
view **manzar**
viewfinder **muhaddid**
   il-manzar
villa **villa**
village **qarya**
vinegar **khall**
violin **kaman/kamanga**
visa **veeza**
visit (noun) **ziyaara;**
   (verb) **yizoor**
visiting hours **mawaаeed**
   iz-ziyaara
visitor **zaayir;**
   (tourist) **saayiн**
voice **soot**
voice mail **risaala**
   sawteyya

W

wait (verb) **yistana,**
   yantazir; *wait!* **istanna!**
waiter (server) **garson;**
   waiter! **ya garson!**
waiting room **ghurfit**
   il-intizaar
Wales **weilz**
walk (noun) **mashey;**
   (verb) **yimshee;** *to go for*
   a walk **yitmashsha**
wall **нeiтa**
wall clock **saaаet нeiтa**
wallet **maнfaza**
want (verb) **аawiz: аawiz/**
   аawza/аawzeen (m/f/pl)
war **нarb**
ward **аanbar**
wardrobe **doolaab**
warm (adj) **daafi**
was: I was **ana kunt;**
   he was **howwa kaan;**
   she was **heyya kaanit;**
   it was **kaan**
watch (noun) **saaаa;**
   (verb) **yoraa'ib**
water (noun) **mayya;**
   (verb) **yis'ee**
water buffalo **gaamoos**
waterfall **shallaal**
waterpipe (for smoking)
   sheesha
wave (noun) **mooga;**
   (verb) **yishaawir**
we **енna**

weather **ig-gaw**
web site **mawqiA Ennit**
wedding **faraH;** wedding anniversary **Aeed zawaag**
Wednesday **(yoom) il-arbaA**
week **usbooA**
welcome **marHaba, ahlan;** you're welcome; (don't mention it) **il-Afw**
Welsh **min weilz**
were: we were **kunna;** you were (m/f/pl) **kunt/ kuntee/kuntoo;** they were **kaanoo**
west **gharb**
wet (adj) **mablool**
what? **eh?**
wheel **Aagala**
wheelchair **kursee lil-muqAadeen;** wheelchair access **ledokhool karaasee beAagal**
when? **imta?**
where? **fein?**
which? **ayy?**
white (adj) (m/f) **abyaD/ beiDa**
who? **meen?**
why? **leh?**
wide (adj) **AreeD**
Wi-Fi code **muftaaH lil-wifi**
wife **zooga**
wind **reeH**
window **shibbaak**
windshield **barabreez**
wine **nibeedh**

wine list **qaa'emit in-nibeedh**
wineglass **kaas**
wing **ginaaH**
with **maAa, bi-**
without **bidoon**
witness **shahid**
woman **sitt, sayyida**
women's restroom **twaalett lis-sayyidaat**
wood **khashab**
wool **soof**
word **kilma**
work (noun) **shughl;** (verb) **yishtaghil**
working (operative) **shagh-ghaal**
world **Aaalam**
worry beads **sibHa**
worse (than) **aw-Hash (min)**
wrapping paper **wara' taghleef**
wrench **muftaaH sawaameel**
wrist **miAsam**
write (verb) **yiktib**
writing paper **wara' lil-kitaaba**
wrong (adj) **khaTa', ghalaT;** wrong number **in-nimra ghalaT**

X, Y, Z

x-ray **soorit il-ashiAa**
yacht **yakht**
year **sana**
yellow (adj) (m/f) **asfar/ safra**

Yemen: South Yemen **ganoob il yaman;** North Yemen **shamaal il yaman**
yes **aywah, naAm**
yesterday **embareH**
yet **lighaayit dilwa'tee;** not yet **lissa**
yogurt **zabaadee**
you (m/f/pl) **enta/enti/ entum;** this is for you **dah Alashaanak** (m), **dah Alashaanik** (f), **dah Alashaankum** (pl); with you **maAaak** (m), **maAaaki** (f), **maAaakum** (pl)
young (adj) **sughayyar (fi es-sin)**
your (m/f/pl) **...-ak/-ik/ kum;** your book (m/f/pl) **kitaabak/kitaabik/ kitaabkum**
yours: is this yours? (m/f/pl) **dah bitaaAak/bitaaAik/ bitaaAkum?**
youth hostel **beit ish-shabaab**
zero **sefr**
zip **sosta**
zoo **Hadeeqit il-Hayawanaat**

Useful Signs

Here are some useful signs you may see around you in the Arabic-speaking world.

دخول	**dukhool** Entrance	خروج	**khuroog** Exit
مفتوح	**maftooH** Open	مغلق	**mughlaq** Closed
ادفع	**idfaA** Push	اسحب	**isHab** Pull
تواليت	**twaalett** Toilet	حمام	**Hammaam** Toilet/bathroom
رجال	**rigaal** Men (restroom)	سيّدات	**sayyidaat** Women (restroom)
مركز الشرطة	**markaz ish-shurTa** Police station	شرطة	**shurTa** Police
مستشفى	**mustashfa** Hospital	طوارئ	**Tawaare'** Emergency
مكتب البريد	**maktab il-bareed** Post office	بنك	**bank** Bank
محطة القطار	**maHaTTit il-aTr** Railroad station	خطر	**khaTar** Danger
للعاملين فقط	**lil Aaamileen faqaT** Staff only		
ممنوع الدخول	**mamnooA id-dukhool** No entry		
ممنوع التصوير	**mamnooA AttaSweer** No photography		
ممنوع التدخين	**mamnooA it-tadkheen** No smoking		

Dialects, script, and grammar

Arabic, which first emerged in the Arabian Peninsula, is now spoken across the MENA region. Modern Standard Arabic (MSA), also known as Fusha Arabic, is the variant taught in schools and used in formal, literary, and academic contexts. All Arabic speakers use MSA when writing, but there are also many spoken dialects that differ greatly in vocabulary, grammar, and pronunciation. The five major dialects are Moroccan, Gulf, Iraqi, Levantine, and Egyptian Arabic—the latter is spoken by over 100 million people and is one of the most widely understood dialects across the MENA region. While the rest of the book teaches Egyptian Arabic, this section offers a basic guide to the Arabic script and grammar using formal MSA. Note that some words you have learned in the book will be spelled, pronounced, and transliterated differently in MSA.

The Arabic alphabet

As with any new script, Arabic takes time and practice to read fluently, but it is not difficult to understand the basic principles or learn how to decipher simple words. In contrast to the Latin alphabet, the Arabic script runs from right to left. There are 28 letters in the Arabic alphabet, and within a word most are joined to each other. The script has no capital letters. Arabic is a phonetic language in which you read what you write since a letter will always have one sound. The letter **alif**, which is the first letter of the alphabet, is the only exception and can be pronounced in a range of different ways—it can represent any short vowel or the longer **aa** sound.

The table below shows all the letters in Arabic in alphabetical order. You can see how their shapes change depending on whether they are separate from any other letter, or are the first, middle, or last letter in a word.

Separated	First	Middle	Last
ا (a)	ا	ل	ل
ب (b)	بـ	ـبـ	ـب
ت (t)	تـ	ـتـ	ـت
ث (th)	ثـ	ـثـ	ـث
ج (j)	جـ	ـجـ	ـج
ح (H)	حـ	ـحـ	ـح
خ (kh)	خـ	ـخـ	ـخ
د (d)	د	ـد	ـد

Separated		First	Middle	Last
ذ	(dh)	ذ	ـذـ	ـذ
ر	(r)	ر	ـر	ـر
ز	(z)	ز	ـز	ـز
س	(s)	سـ	ـسـ	ـس
ش	(sh)	شـ	ـسـ	ـس
ص	(s)	صـ	ـصـ	ـص
ض	(D)	ضـ	ـضـ	ـض
ط	(T)	ط	ـطـ	ـط
ظ	(z)	ظ	ـظـ	ـظ
ع	(A)	عـ	ـعـ	ـع
غ	(gh)	غـ	ـغـ	ـغ
ف	(f)	فـ	ـفـ	ـف
ق	(q)	قـ	ـقـ	ـق
ك	(k)	كـ	ـكـ	ـك
ل	(l)	لـ	ـلـ	ـل
م	(m)	مـ	ـمـ	ـم
ن	(n)	نـ	ـنـ	ـن
ه	(h)	هـ	ـهـ	ـه
و	(w)	و	ـو	ـو
ي	(y, ee)	يـ	ـيـ	ـي

Letter shapes

The Arabic alphabet is derived from geometric figures such as triangles, circles, or combinations of both. It consists of 18 shapes that express 28 phonetic sounds.

Eighteen of the 28 Arabic letters are the same shape as one or more other letters, and are only distinguished by dots above or below them. These dots are an integral part of the letter, just like the dot of the "j" or the cross of the "t", and should not be confused with the optional vowel marks (pp.156). You can see the similarity between the following groups or pairs of letters.

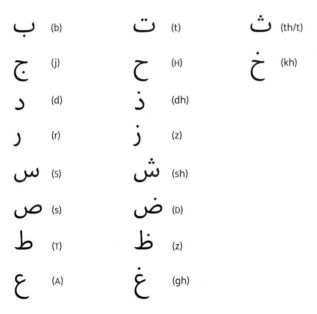

ب (b)   ت (t)   ث (th/t)

ج (j)   ح (H)   خ (kh)

د (d)   ذ (dh)

ر (r)   ز (z)

س (s)   ش (sh)

ص (s)   ض (D)

ط (T)   ظ (z)

ع (A)   غ (gh)

Each of the remaining ten letters of the Arabic alphabet has a unique shape, but some letters look like others when they are joined to other letters within a word.

ا (a)   ف (f)   ق (q)   ك (k)

ل (l)   م (m)   ن (n)   ه (h)

و (w/oo)   ي (y/ee)

Joining letters

Arabic writing is cursive, or "joined up," and is only rarely written as separate letters—for example, in a crossword. All 28 letters can be joined to the letter before them in a word, and all but six can be joined to the letter after them. The shape of a letter changes when it is joined to others, but it still retains enough features to make it recognizable. In general, when an Arabic letter is joined to the letter after it (to the left), it loses any left-hand tail or flourish it has when on its own. It still, however, keeps any dots above or below it, to distinguish it from other letters of the same shape. Look at the examples below, read from right to left.

فجر (fajr/dawn) = ر (r) + ج (j) + ف (f)

مصر (misr/Egypt) = ر (r) + ص (s) + م (m)

عند (Aend/at) = د (d) + ن (n) + ع (a)

طبق (Tabaq/dish) = ق (q) + ب (b) + ط (t)

فيه (feeh/in it) = ه (h) + ي (y/ee) + ف (f)

سبت (sabt/Saturday) = ت (t) + ب (b) + س (s)

Note how the shapes of the letters ع (**A**), غ (**gh**), ك (**k**), and ه (**h**) change when they are joined to another letter.

مع (maAa/with) = ع (A) + م (m)

مغر (mughre/tempting) = ر (r) + غ (gh) + م (m)

سكر (sukkar/sugar) = ر (r) + ك (k) + س (s)

كل (kul/all) = ل (l) + ك (k)

نهر (nahr/river) = ر (r) + ه (h) + ن (n)

هي (heya/she) = ي (y/ee) + ه (h)

You will notice that the shape of most Arabic letters, when joined to other letters in a word, depends on their position in the word: first, middle, or last. When a letter comes last in a word, it usually has a "tail" or some kind of flourish. For example, the letters س (**s**) and ش (**sh**) have a left-hand tail, but lose this when not the last letter, leaving just the small "w" shape (with three dots above for **sh**).

آسف (**aasif**/sorry) = ف (f) + س (s) + آ (aa)

مارس (**maaris**/March) = س (s) + ر (r) + ا (aa) + م (m)

شاحن (**shaaHin**/charger) = ن (n) + ح (H) + ا (aa) + ش (sh)

The six letters that are never joined to any letter after them—ا (**a**), د (**d**), ذ (**dh/z**), ر (**r**), ز (**z**), and و (**w/oo**)—always have a space between them and the next letter. This makes them easier to recognize as they don't significantly change their shapes.

انت (**anta**/you) = ت (t) + ن (n) + ا (aa)

دار (**dar**/home) = ر (r) + ا (aa) + د (d)

زوج (**zawg**/husband) = ج (j) + و (w/oo) + ز (z)

اب (**ab**/father) = ب (b) + ا (aa)

The hamza and other additional marks

The hamza is a small sign that can appear above or below other letters, or by itself (ء). It represents a glottal stop (as if *butter* was said as "bu'er"), but is not strongly pronounced in spoken Arabic. It can sometimes be heard as a small pause in the middle of a word, similar to the spoken pronunciation of ق (**q**).

أب (**ab**/father)

مائدة (**maa'ida**/table)

In modern written Arabic, many vowels are not written as letters. However, short vowels and double letters may be indicated by diacritics—which native speakers leave out when writing—above and (in one case) below the script.

ـَ = a   ـُ = u/o   ـِ = i/e   ـّ = double letter

Look at the elements that make up the Arabic word **mumkin** (*possible*), which is written as "**mmkn**," and the alternative written forms with and without vowels.

$$\text{م} + \text{م} + \text{ك} + \text{ن} = \text{ممكن} \ \text{or} \ \text{مُمكِن}$$

Similarly, in the word **qamar** (*moon*), the **-a** sound should be represented by a diacritic (قَمَر), but will usually be written without it (قمر). Some more examples of such words are given below.

مَحَطّة or محطة (**maнaтта**/station)

بُرج or برج (**borj**/tower)

Double letters, such as in the word **maнaтта** above, are indicated by the shadda diacritic, meaning that the same letter is pronounced twice in a row—the first time like a consonant and the second time in accordance with the sound of the vowel following it. For example, the word **sayyida** (*lady*) is pronounced **sai** then **yida**.

Most modern written Arabic assumes that the reader is familiar with the pronunciation, and this can make reading the script challenging for learners. However, most beginners find that reading Arabic without vowel marks becomes easier with practice, as the patterns of the language become more familiar. Look back at some of the words and phrases in this book and see if you can work out the Arabic script using the alphabet table on pp.152–153 and the pronunciation guide given in the lessons.

The feminine ending

In Arabic, the feminine ending **-a** is written as a circle with two dots above, like a cross between the letters ه (**h**) and ت (**t**): ة. This is called **taa marbooтa**, "tied-up T", because it can also be pronounced **-t** or **-it** when placed in certain word combinations—for example, غرفة (**ghurfa**/room), but غرفة الأولاد (**ghurfit il-awlaad**/the children's room).

تذكرة (**tazkara**/ticket)

تذكرتين (**tazkartayn**/two tickets)

زوجة (**zawga**/wife)

زوجة أمير (**zawgat ameer**/Amir's wife)

Plurals

Some Arabic words can be made plural by adding one of two endings: **-aat** or **-een**, as in **hammaam/hammaamaat** (*bathroom/bathrooms*) or **muwazzaf/muwazzafeen** (*employee/employees*). However, many other plurals are made by altering the vowel sounds within a word, as occurs in English with goose/geese or mouse/mice. Examples of this type of plural include **layla/leyaalee** (*night/nights*), **ghurfa/ghuraf** (*room/rooms*), and **tifl/aTfaal** (*child/children*). You will need to learn these plurals individually.

The definite article: al

There are two types of letters in the Arabic alphabet: ت (**t**), ث (**th**), د (**d**), ذ (**dh**), س (**s**), ش (**sh**), ص (**S**), ض (**D**), ط (**T**), ظ (**z**), ل (**l**), and ن (**n**) are known as Shamsi letters, while the rest are known as Qamari letters. These determine the pronunciation of the definite article **al** (MSA), used as a prefix with Arabic words. If the first letter of the word following **al** is Shamsi, the sound **-l** changes to become the sound of that letter – for example, الشمس (**ash-shams**/*the sun*) or السمكة (**as-samaka**/*the fish*). On the other hand, if the first letter after **al** is Qamari, the **-l** is fully pronounced – for example, القمر (**al-qamar**/*the moon*) or الكلب (**al-kalb**/*the dog*). In both of these cases, the script is not affected.

Numbers

In Arabic script, 1 and 9 are easily recognizable, but other numbers look quite different. A zero is written as a dot.

٠ (صفر/**Sefr**/zero)

١ (واحد/**waaHid**/one)

٢ (اثنين/**itnein**/two)

٣ (ثلاثة/**talaata**/three)

٤ (أربعة/**arbaAa**/four)

١٠ (عشرة/**Aashra**/ten)

٥ (خمسة/**khamsa**/five)

٦ (ستة/**sitta**/six)

٧ (سبعة/**sabAa**/seven)

٨ (ثمانية/**tamanya**/eight)

٩ (تسعة/**tisAa**/nine)

١٠٠٠ (ألف/**alf**/thousand)

Acknowledgments

FOURTH EDITION (2024)
For this edition, the publisher would like to thank Shipra Jain for design assistance; Manpreet Kaur and Deepak Negi for picture research assistance; Jake Bergamin for the editorial review; Peter Bull Art Studio and Gus Scott for additional illustrations; and Andiamo! Language Services Ltd for foreign language proofreading.

THIRD EDITION (2018)
Senior Editors Angela Wilkes, Christine Stroyan; **Art Editor** Hugh Schermuly; **Designer** Mitun Banerjee; **DTP Designer** Pushpak Tyagi; **Senior DTP Coordinator** Sunil Sharma; **Jacket Design Development Manager** Sophia MTT; **Jacket Designer** Juhi Sheth; **Pre-Producer** David Almond; **Senior Producer** Alex Bell; **Publisher** Liz Wheeler; **Publishing Director** Jonathan Metcalf; **Special Photography** Mike Good, Marcus Wilson-Smith

FIRST EDITION (2009)
The publisher would like to thank the following for their help in the preparation of this book: Abu Zaad Restaurant, Shepherd's Bush; Magnet Showroom, Enfield, London; MyHotel, London; Peppermint Green Hairdressers, London; Capel Manor College; The Savoy Hotel, Sharm El Sheikh; Richard Simmons; Jane Gibbon and Max.

The publisher would also like to thank the following people who appear as models: Ahmed Mahmoud Mubarak; Heidi Kirolos; Mahitab El A'war; Mai Kholief; Mahmoud El Beleidy; Haneen El-Beih; Amina Mansour; Abdelrahman Ayman Helry; Mena Talla Hassan El Menabawy; Hayat Kamil; Pia Noor; Neelpa Odedra; Adam Brackenbury; Silke Spingies; Mini Vhra; Adam Walker; Martha Evatt; Mehdi Khandan; Michael Duffy; Sue Alniab; Jason Carnegie; Abdullah Akhazzan; Mahmoud Gafaar.

Language content for Dorling Kindersley by g-and-w publishing; **Managed by** Jane Wightwick; **Editing and additional input** Cathy Gaulter-Carter, Teresa Cervera, Leila Gaafar; **Additional editorial assistance** Lynn Bresler; **Picture research** Schermuly Design Co

PICTURE CREDITS

Key: a-above; b-below/bottom; c-centre; f-far; l-left; r-right; t-top

1 Getty Images / iStock: Ugurhan. **2 Dreamstime.com:** Oleh Panasenko (br). **Shutterstock.com:** Igor Chus (tr). **3 Alamy Stock Photo:** Hemis / Dozier Marc (br). **Dreamstime.com:** Vrovel (tr). **Getty Images / iStock:** E+ / Fat Camera (tl); Dave Primov (bl). **8 Getty Images / iStock:** Prostock Studio (cr). **9 Getty Images / iStock:** Creative Credit (tl). **10 Dreamstime.com:** Lacheev (crb). **Getty Images / iStock:** Baona (cb/Brother); shapecharge (cb). **11 Shutterstock.com:** ildintorlak (tl). **12 Getty Images / iStock:** E+ / Fat Camera (cr). **13 Dreamstime.com:** Yuri Arcurs (cla). **Getty Images / iStock:** E+ / Orbon Alija (clb); monkeybusinessimages (cl). **Shutterstock.com:** Prostock-studio (br). **14 Ingram Image Library:** (cra); **Grapheast** (crb); **Dreamstime.com:** Yuri Arcurs (crb); Prostockstudio (crb/Boss). **15 Dreamstime.com:** Arne9001 (cl). **Getty Images / iStock:** E+ / GCShutter (bl); Don White (cla). **Shutterstock.com:** Drazen Zigic (clb/Student). **17 Dreamstime.com:** Lacheev (bl). **Getty Images / iStock:** Baona (bc/Brother); shapecharge (bc). **Shutterstock.com:** ildintorlak (ca). **18 Getty Images / iStock:** Berenika_L (cb). **18-19 Getty Images / iStock:** FabrikaCr (c). **19 Dreamstime.com:** Gpointstudio (cb); Ramzi Hachicho (tl); Pretoperola (tc); Vrovel (c). **21 Shutterstock.com:** LightField Studios (tl). **22 Dreamstime.com:** Lee Avison (crb); Jianghongyan (ca); Chris Dorney (ca/Peppers); Kkovaleva (ca/ Zucchini). **Getty Images / iStock:** E+ / Floortje (c/Cheese); Alasdair James (c); etiennevoss (c/Feta). **23 Dreamstime.com:** Ab2147272 (clb). **24 Alamy Stock Photo:** Prostock-studio (bl). **Getty Images / iStock:** Rafinade (cr). **25 Dreamstime.com:** Michael Lunceford (cla); Okea (tl). **Getty Images / iStock:** monkeybusinessimages (bl); ShotShare (cl). **26 Getty Images / iStock:** Berenika_L (bc); Kuppa_rock (tr); FabrikaCr (br). **Shutterstock.com:** Prostock-studio (cr). **27 Dreamstime.com:** Lee Avison (tl); Okea (ca). **Getty Images / iStock:** E+ / Floortje (cla/Cheese); Alasdair James (cla); etiennevoss (cla/Feta). **28 Alamy Stock Photo:** Colinspics (cr). **Dreamstime.com:** Fizkes (crb). **Getty Images / iStock:** E+ / Koh Sze Kiat (br). **29 Alamy Stock Photo:** PhotoAlto / Michele Constantini (bl). **Getty Images / iStock:** E+ / xavierarnau (clb). **iStockphoto. com:** Philippa Banks (cl). **30 Dreamstime.com:** Syda Productions (crb). Comstock Images (br). **31 Getty Images / iStock:** E+ / mihailomilovanovic (cl). **32 Dreamstime.com:** Fizkes (cr). **33 Dreamstime.com:** Prostockstudio (crb). **Getty Images / iStock:** E+ / mbbirdy (tl, cl); E+ / GCShutter (cla). **34 Dreamstime.com:** Roman Egorov (c). **Getty Images:** fStop / Halfdark (cr). **Shutterstock.com:** Araddara (cb). **34-35 Dreamstime. com:** Jiri Hera (ca). **35 Dreamstime.com:** Yuri Arcurs (tc); Fizkes (cb); Aldo Di Bari Murga (cl). **Getty Images / iStock:** E+ / SrdjanPav (ca); E+ / WillSelarep (ca/Businesswoman). **36 Dreamstime.com:** Roman Egorov (cla); Aldo Di Bari Murga (ca). **36-37 Dreamstime.com:** Jiri Hera (tc). **37 Dreamstime.com:** Okea (cb). **Getty Images / iStock:** fStop / Halfdark (cla). **Getty Images / iStock:** Rafinade (bl). **38 Shutterstock.com:** Mltz (cr). **39 Getty Images / iStock:** E+ / FatCamera (tl); studio529 (cb). **40 Dreamstime.com:** Anton Aleksenko (cr). **Getty Images / iStock:** Mystockimages (bl). **41 Dreamstime.com:** Artzzz (clb/Bus); Robert Paul Van Beets (tl); Repazz (cl); Kinglau (clb). **Shutterstock.com:** Marwa M. Dakhakhny (bl); SRStudio (cl/Taxi). **43 Dreamstime.com:** Anton Aleksenko (cla); Robert Paul Van Beets (cb). **Getty Images / iStock:** LUke1138 (cl); Ugurhan (tl). **44-45 Shutterstock.com:** Nerthuz (c). **45 Getty Images:** Tom Dulat / Stringer (cla). **Getty Images / iStock:** Tramino (tl). **46 Dreamstime. com:** Kinglau (br); Repazz (cra). **Getty Images / iStock:** Joel Carillet (ca). **Shutterstock.com:** Nerthuz (tc); SRStudio (cra/Taxi). **47 Dreamstime.com:** Robert Paul Van Beets (cla). **Shutterstock.com:** Marwa M. Dakhakhny (bl). **48-49 Dreamstime.com:** Evgeniy Fesenko (c). **48 Alamy Stock Photo:** imageBROKER.com GmbH & Co. KG / Heiner Heine (bc). **Dreamstime.com:** David Steele (br). **Getty Images / iStock:** LUke1138 (cb/Museum); onfilm (cb). **49 Shutterstock.com:** Igor Chus (tl); Curioso.Photography (tl). **50-51 Dreamstime.com:** Evgeniy Fesenko (c). **51 Dreamstime.com:** Kittichai Boonpong (cb/Background); Andrey Popov (cb). **53 Alamy Stock Photo:** Image Farm Inc. / James Dawson (cla/Disabled). **Dreamstime.com:** Claudiodivizia (tl); Giovanni Gagliardi (cla). **54 Dreamstime.com:** Fizkes (br). **Getty Images / iStock:** Audy_indy (crb); Akarawut Lohacharoenvanich (cr). **55 Dreamstime.com:** Aprescindere (clb/tickets); Nadezhda1906 (cla). **Getty Images / iStock:** E+ / andresr (clb); xavierarnau (tl); E+ / izusek (bl). **56-57 Shutterstock.com:** Nerthuz (b). **56 Dreamstime.com:** Dinatemraz (ca/ Market); Evgeniy Fesenko (tr); David Steele (c). **Getty Images / iStock:** LUke1138 (ca). **Shutterstock.com:** Igor Chus (tc). **58 Dreamstime.com:** David Brooks (crb). **Getty Images / iStock:** 0802290022 (cra); Kwangmoozaa (cr); E+ / zeljkosantrac (crb/Family). **59 iStockphoto.com:** vera bogaerts (tl). **60 Getty Images / iStock:** AlexandrBognat (cb); Yastrebinsky (crb); DNY59 (crb/Towel). **Shutterstock.com:** Sarymsakov Andrey (cr). **61 Getty Images / iStock:** Kanawa_Studio (cl); yipengge (tl). Image Source Pink (cl). Ingram Image Library (clb). **62-63 Alamy Stock Photo:** Hemis / Dozier Marc (c). **64 Dreamstime.com:** Oleh Panasenko (br). **65 Alamy Stock Photo:** Arcaid Images / Richard Bryant (clb/Wash basin). **Dreamstime.com:** Apiwan Borrikonratchata (cla). **Getty Images / iStock:** Eva-Katalin (clb); KanchitDon (tl). **Shutterstock.com:** Shaima Mamdouh Elshamy (cla/Traffic). **66 Alamy Stock Photo:** Arcaid Images / Richard Bryant (ca). **Getty Images / iStock:** AlexandrBognat (cb/Slippers); Yastrebinsky (cb); DNY59 (crb). **66-67 Shutterstock.com:** Sarymsakov Andrey (b). **67 Dreamstime.com:** Dmitrii Melnikov (ca). **Getty Images / iStock:** KanchitDon (bc). **68 Alamy Stock Photo:** Eye Ubiquitous / Bennett Dean (cr); Peter Horree (c). **Getty Images / iStock:** DKart (cb); GarySandyWales (ca). **Shutterstock.com:** Official (cra). **69 Dreamstime.com:** Marcel De Grijs (cl). **Getty Images / iStock:** nastya_ph (tl); prill (cla). **Alamy Stock Photo:** Bartomeu Amengual (clb). **70-71 Alamy Stock Photo:** Design Pics / Radius Images (c). **71 Getty Images / iStock:** E+ / GoodLifeStudio (c). **72 Dreamstime.com:** Chuyu (cb); Ovydyborets (cb/Cabbage); Kkovaleva (cb/Zucchini); Jianghongyan (cb/Spinach); Ilyach (bl). **73 Dreamstime.com:** Chernetskaya (tl); Andrey Mikhaylov (cl); Ulga (clb). **Getty Images / iStock:** E+ / Drazen_ (cla). **Alamy Stock Photo:** Nick Hanna (tl). **74 Dreamstime.com:** Pressmaster (cr). **Getty Images:** DigitalVision / EMS-FORSTER-PRODUCTIONS (bl). **75 Getty Images / iStock:** leolintang (br). **76 Alamy Stock Photo:** Design Pics / Radius Images (cra); Peter Horree (br). **Dreamstime.com:** Marcel De Grijs (crb). **Getty Images / iStock:** DKart (cb); GarySandyWales (cb/Bakery). **Shutterstock.com:** Official (bc/Cakes). **77 Dreamstime.com:** Chuyu (cla); Jianghongyan (cla/Spinach). **78 Dreamstime.com:** Liubomyr Vorona (br). **Getty Images / iStock:** E+ / RealPeopleGroup (c). **79 Getty Images / iStock:** E+ / shapecharge (tl, cla, cla/ Businessmen, clb). **Shutterstock.com:** Zhu Difeng (bl). **80 Getty Images / iStock:** E+ / Koh Sze Kiat (cra). **80-81 Getty Images:** Rob Melnychuk (cb). **82 Dreamstime.com:** Pressmaster (cra); Repazz (crbb). **iStockphoto.com:** Mark Kostich (cr). Ingram Image Library (crb). **83 Shutterstock.com:** Abie Davies (tl). **84-85 Shutterstock.com:** Pressmaster (c). **84 Shutterstock.com:** Goncharov_Artem (bl). **85 Dreamstime.com:** Vinnstock (bc). **Getty Images / iStock:** LUHUANFENG (cb); PeopleImages (tc, ca). **Shutterstock.com:** Drazen Zigic (c). **86 Dreamstime. com:** Liubomyr Vorona (br). **87 Dreamstime.com:** Gpointstudio (bc). **Getty Images / iStock:** Fabrika Cr (bl). **89 Dreamstime.com:** Aaron Amat (cb). **Getty Images / iStock:** E+ / andresr (bl); fizkes (tl). **90 Dreamstime.com:** Chernetskaya (cb). **91 Getty Images / iStock:** E+ / damircudic (tl). **92 Getty Images / iStock:** E+ / FatCamera (cr). **93 Getty Images / iStock:** DigitalVision / Morsa Images (tl). **94 Dreamstime.com:** Rido (br). **Getty Images / iStock:** E+ / Morsa Images (cra). **95 Dreamstime.com:** Shawn Hempel (clb). **Getty Images / iStock:** LattaPictures (tl); seb_ra (clb/Doctor). **97 Dreamstime.com:** Pressmaster (t). **Getty Images / iStock:** DigitalVision / Morsa Images (b). **98-99 Dreamstime.com:** Arsty (c). **98 Dreamstime.com:** Pv Productions (bl). **99 Getty Images / iStock:** E+ / CreativaStudio (c); mapo (tl); Kwangmoozaa (tc). **Shutterstock.com:** Ersler Dmitry (bc). **100 Dreamstime. com:** Draftmode (cb). **Getty Images / iStock:** sihuo0860371 (cr). **102 Dreamstime.com:** Frogtravel (cr). **102-103 Getty Images / iStock:** brytta (b). **103 Dreamstime.com:** Welcomia (cla). **Getty Images / iStock:** E+ / Nikada (tl). **iStockphoto.com** (c). **104 Dreamstime.com:** Celiavegaa (ca); Yevheniia Sednieva (cb); Missjelena (br). **104-105 Dreamstime.com:** Duncan Noakes (c). **105 123RF.com:** Mladen Mitrinovic (bl). **Getty Images / iStock:** lukyeee1976 (c). **106-107 Getty Images / iStock:** sihuo0860371 (bc). **106 Dreamstime.com:** Draftmode (bc). **107 Getty Images / iStock:** E+ / CreativaStudio (cl); E+ / Nikada (bc). **108 Getty Images / iStock:** E+ / ultramarinfoto (cr); Dave Primov (crb). **109 Getty Images / iStock:** mediaphotos (cla). **110 Getty Images / iStock:** LumiNola (cr). **111 Dreamstime.com:** Albertshakirov (clb). **Getty Images / iStock:** nilimage (tl). **112 Getty Images / iStock:** E+ / BraunS (bl). **Shutterstock.com:** Marwa M. Dakhakhny (cr). **113 Dreamstime.com:** Diego Vito Cervo (tl); Chernetskaya (bl). **Getty Images / iStock:** OJO Images / Sam Edwards (clb). **114 Dreamstime.com:** Amsis1 (br); Yuliia Kaveshnikova (cr); Brett Critchley (crb); Satel22 (br/Money). **115 Dreamstime.com:** Presse750 (br). **Getty Images / iStock:** E+ / Juanmonino (c); poco_bw (cla); E+ / Pekic (clb). **116 Dreamstime.com:** Diego Vito Cervo (c). **Getty Images / iStock:** E+ / ultramarinfoto (cb/Sea); Dave Primov (cb); mediaphotos (br). **Shutterstock.com:** Marwa M. Dakhakhny (cr). **117 Getty Images / iStock:** E+ / Juanmonino (c). **118-119 Shutterstock.com:** Orhan Cam (c). **119 Dreamstime.com:** Prostockstudio (cb). **120 Dreamstime.com:** Mikhail Kokhanchikov (cb); Zavgsg (cr). **Shutterstock.com:** Amir Elsayed (br). **121 Shutterstock.com:** Romeo Koitmäe (tl). **122-123 Dreamstime.com:** Monkey Business Images (c). **123 Getty Images / iStock:** adisa (tl). **124 Dreamstime.com:** Celiavegaa (cra); Yevheniia Sednieva (c); Zavgsg (crb); Mikhail Kokhanchikov (cb); Skypixel (cb/Basketball); Sergeyoch (cb/Ball); Volkop (bc). **124-125 Dreamstime.com:** Duncan Noakes (tc)

All other images © Dorling Kindersley